NAPOLEON'S WAR MAXIMS.

NAPOLEON'S WAR MAXIMS

WITH HIS

SOCIAL AND POLITICAL THOUGHTS

BY

PROFESSOR L. E. HENRY, B.A., M.R.C.P.,
University of Cambridge and Oxford Union Society,

LATE

Reader to H.R.H. The Duke of Clarence,
Professor at the Royal Staff College, Sandhurst,
Examiner at the Royal Military Academy, Woolwich,
Membre correspondant de l'Académie de Clermont-Ferrand,
de la Société de Topographie Nationale de France,
de la Société Bibliographique de Paris, et de l'Union Faulconnier,
Société Historique de Dunkerque,
ARMY AND DIPLOMACY TUTOR.

The Naval & Military Press Ltd

Published by

The Naval & Military Press Ltd
Unit 5 Riverside, Brambleside
Bellbrook Industrial Estate
Uckfield, East Sussex
TN22 1QQ England

Tel: +44 (0)1825 749494

www.naval-military-press.com
www.nmarchive.com

In reprinting in facsimile from the original, any imperfections are inevitably reproduced and the quality may fall short of modern type and cartographic standards.

THIS BOOK

IS

WITH HIS ROYAL HIGHNESS'S SPECIAL PERMISSION

Respectfully Dedicated

BY THE WRITER'S WISH

TO

HIS ROYAL HIGHNESS

PRINCE ALBERT VICTOR OF WALES,

DUKE OF CLARENCE AND AVONDALE, K.G.,

Major of the 10th Royal Hussars,

WITH WHOM HE WORKED

AND

WHOSE ROYAL FRIENDSHIP HE GREATLY

VALUED.

PREFACE.

KNOWLEDGE *practical* and *active*, to be made an obligatory qualification in both the Teacher and the Student, is the one means in the case of Officers the most likely to solve the riddle of English growlers who repeat urgently the cry of "The Army as a Profession!" "Military Examinations!" and "Why should we join the Militia?" And an early repeal of the curse of short service and less coddling in the case of the rank-and-file will prove an instantaneous cure against physical and moral degeneration afloat and ashore.

Cambridge and Oxford Professors may be forgiven their a trifle exclusive and a little dreary teaching; a forbidding individuality the knowing and unctuous University Professor is by profession. But Military and Naval Instructors should be willing men, neither excluding theorists nor dormant teachers. Therefore the training of our Military and Naval Officers must be, before all else, *practical* and *active*, though skilled at the same time, *cela s'entend.* For this motive— and here it gives me pleasure to thank my just and ever-kind Commanding Officer at the Staff College, General EDWARD CLIVE, for his ready support in the matter at Head Quarters— I it was who introduced the practical *Aide Mémoire de l'Officier d'État-Major en Campagne* into the course of our French studies, along with never ceasing to speak French with my Students, always translating into French at sight at lectures, and with a French dissertation weekly. I consider different teaching a fraud. I call that cheating the State of a salary, and an iniquitous harm is being done to the Officer eventually. Let us be practical then.

PREFACE.

Competitive Examinations—people seem to forget the fact at the present day—are the outcome of the jaundiced jealousy from the moneyed Middle Classes against Aristocracy and Gentry, in whose hands the chosen professions of Church, Army, Navy and Diplomacy have remained an honoured privilege—and justly so. I say "justly so;" for, the Army and Navy, equally with the Diplomacy, should remain officered by men born and bred *gentlemen*. Indeed the rank and file are intelligent enough to tell you *who* is *who* from their officers. My readers, who have met in the same services as myself, will not call me an insolent man for so plain an opinion as mine, I make sure ; and outsiders know nothing of the absolute necessity for an officer of the British Navy or Army to be—give me leave to say—exclusively a man well-born and well-bred. The money bag and book learning do not make a man what Englishmen call a *gentleman*. Leave then the skilled work to specialists, whose train of thought will set difficult matters right ahead ; the rest of the officers will do well enough on the field of battle, though less attentive to book work and more imaginary, maybe. England's Naval and Military Registers of pre-Competitive-Examination-days are remarkable enough and sufficiently stirring to drive me mad at the weakening attempts—powerless, Heaven be praised !—of Socialistico-Democratic Reformers after breaking up the solid and beneficial system of having men at the head of the Army, Navy, or Diplomacy, who are not *bourgeois*. I am speaking of this Century only : Who and what were the Diplomats, the Military and the Naval Officers who got England through so gallantly and so successfully ? The *gentlemen* of Old England—Abercromby, Nelson, Wellesley, Whitelock, Cathcart, Moore, Graham, Beresford, Hill, Cotton, Sir J. Murray, Exmouth, Hastings (1817), Hislop (1817), Keane, Napier, Hardinge, Smith (of Aliwal), Gough (of Sobraon, and Chilianwallah), Lord Raglan (of Alma fame), Lord Lucan and Lord Cardigan (of Balaklava), Sir George Cathcart, Strangways, Goldie and

Torrens (of Inkerman), the victorious leaders of Indian Mutiny name, and lastly the present good old Duke of Cambridge. Heroes of Naval renown — numerous as "the beautiful stars in Heaven so bright"—I will not undertake to name.* Old-fashioned readers of this book will find it an agreeable object lesson of how English gentlemen of pre-Competitive-Examination-days always did their duty everywhere on sea as on land if they read well the very small (only 37 pp. in 8vo.) account of the career of the brave Naval Officer, Captain ROBERT HAY, Commander of the H.E.I.G's Ship "Astell," together with some further particulars of his life and of his sons, written by the gallant officer's good and patriotic daughter, Miss Leonora E. Hay, of Malvern Wells, and dedicated to his learned grandson, Mr. Alexander HAY-TOD of Charter House School at Godalming.

As to the Diplomatic Service, enough to say that British Diplomacy maintains not the dogma of Papal Infallibility. True. But the healthy honesty of English Diplomatic and Consular Representatives abroad has brought enough sincere friendships with "substantial" additions towards the Queen's Realm that the restive "Republican-Monarchists" of England and her restless *forwards* Reformers—Semi-lunar Sentimentalists cranky or in ill health—are content to confess, without reticence, that Lord Salisbury is not wrong in restricting Diplomatic Representation to English gentlemen. From 1806, under Lord Grenville, Mr. Charles J. Fox, and Viscount Howick, down to 1874, under Lord Beaconsfield, Earl Derby, and the Marquis of Salisbury, British Diplomacy has thriven well enough, though the Foreign Office remains the Foreign Secretary's "Preserves."

Speaking of national omens and writing as a Frenchman, I cannot help feeling that the English will fare better as a nation and as individuals if they will return to their pre-Competitive-Examination-days. Unfortunately, the alli-

* Read "Logs of the Great Sea Fights, 1794—1805" of England, by Rear-Admiral T. STURGESS JACKSON (Vol. I., *Navy Records Society*). (L. E. H.)

ance between Plutocracy and Prolétariat is likely to degrade England if Socialism be encouraged further by those who call themselves "Republican - Monarchist" Englishmen. What France is passing through because of her violation of traditional rights is a warning of no tender meaning. Revolution has been put in motion ; a defender of Monarchy is a hostile power to a Frenchman non-Royalist ; perpetual are the intestine disputes within the Republican sets between the *arrivés* and the *affamés*. What next ? Fire and Death. Alas ! that "jaundiced jealousy ! " It is because of their jaundiced jealousy of Monarchy that French Republicans and Imperialists—Siamese twins as they are—would prefer a new war with Germany or England to "putting up the shutters" at the *palais de l'Elysée*. Preventing the Princes of the Royal Family of France from taking their due place and proper share in that country's affairs, and thereby gaining that popularity with the Army and the Nation which they would naturally acquire : this is their one idea and care. The Imperialists did the same thing when War was declared between France and Germany in 1870. On that day, it is notable, all the members of the Royal Family of France addressed, from Brussels, letters to the French Government offering to fight in defence of their country. The Prince DE JOINVILLE wrote to Admiral Rigault de Genouilly, the French Minister of Marine :—" In presence of the danger which threatens our country, I ask the emperor to be allowed to serve in the active army in any capacity, and request my old comrade to help me to obtain this leave."—The Duke D' AUMALE wrote to the Minister for War :—" You are calling out all Frenchmen to fight for the defence of the country. I am a Frenchman, a soldier fit for duty, and am a General of Division. I ask to serve in the active army." The Duke DE CHARTRES wrote :—" As a Frenchman, and as a former Officer in the American and Italian Wars, I request to be employed on active service. My most ardent wish is to fight for my country, even if it be only as a Volunteer."—*Braves enfants de la France!* For obvious reasons these Royal offers were declined. But I cannot help confessing I do not think Republican France is at present nearly strong enough for such a war. And, on the other hand, the Princes may not bear being exiled for much longer if they have not turned cowards. 1870—1871 are two dates of dejected memory to Frenchmen, and to a Frenchman not venal such a memory is ever exciting his love, as towards a suffering mother. A mother is never dearer to one as when one sees her torn with mental anguish or physical pain, is she? So it is with the French Princes, whose experience has made them more logical and less loquacious than the present Rulers of France. These Princes of the Royal Family of France remembered this well: *La patrie, c'est la mère d'un peuple passant à travers les siècles.*

Knowledge *practical* and *active* is then the one means, the one most likely to solve the riddle of growing discontent, as expressed in the Press by parents coveting the chosen professions for their sons, and who reproach their "Republican-Monarchist" friends with saying such a lot and doing so little. *Toujours la fable du Juge et des Plaideurs, n'est-ce pas?*

It is then and only in view to being a practical teacher that I am publishing this book about so essentially and so pre-eminently practical a soldier as Napoléon. The French are warmhearted enough and with generous impulses; the difficulty is to get at those among them who can rise superior to narrow national prejudices, and who are so much citizens of the world as to recognise merit wherever they find it. Though I am a French Royalist, I found the great Napoléon a perfect type as a soldier; and next I supposed that my officers-students, and other military and naval thinkers would contemplate over Napoléon's practical "mind" as fondly as I did. Hence this my present anatomic study of that great warrior of undying fame. But as a political and social leader, Napoléon was not a "success"; *usurpers* never are—and these must not be allowed to come into existence either. What else was Napoléon but that? He it was who said of himself: *Je suis la Révolution!* Harm hatch, harm catch then.

An undertaking exclusively military has necessarily called for consultations with military friends and colleagues. And I would here express especially my obligations to Colonel E. CLAYTON, R.A., P.S.C., late Professor of Fortifications and Artillery, Staff College, and Colonel on the Staff at Head Quarters of South Eastern District, for his assistance, and thank him for his most courteous and invaluable co-operation. I have much confidence that Colonel Clayton's useful military suggestions have conduced to the greater trustworthiness of this Book as fairly useful, before all others, to the great body of the British and American Military Public.

LUCIEN HENRY.

September 8th, 1899.

CONTENTS.

	PAGE
PREFACE	vii
INTRODUCTORY LETTER	1

PART I.
WAR MAXIMS.

BOOK I.	17
BOOK II.	39

PART II.
ILLUSTRATION OF THE MAXIMS.

BOOK I.	48

PART III.

THOUGHTS RELATIVE TO THE ART OF WAR ...	129

PART IV.
SOCIAL AND POLITICAL THOUGHTS.

INTRODUCTORY REMARKS	138
BOOK I.	147
BOOK II.	161

CONCLUSION AND BOOKS OF REFERENCE	183

TABLES OF CONTENTS.

I. METHODICAL TABLE OF MAXIMS.

Principles of War ... vi, vii, x, xi, xvi, xviii, xxiii, xxiv, xxv, xxvi, xxvii, xxviii, xxix, xxxiii, xxxiv, lv, lxxvii, lxxviii, lxxxiv, xcv, xcvi, xcvii, cii, civ, cv, cxii

War of Method	v
War of Marches and Counter Marches ...	xvii
War of Offensive and Defensive ...	vii, xiv, xix, ci
War of Moral	cxiii, cxiv
Plan of Campaign ...	ii
Line of Operation ...	xii, xx
Frontiers	i
Organization of an Army ...	lvii
Marches of an Army	iii, iv, vi, ix, ix, xxi, xxiii, civ
Flank ...	xxx, cvi
Army Corps on Marches	xiii
Command	lxiv, lxvi
General-in-Chief	viii, xv, xxxi, lxiii, lxv, lxvi, lxx, lxxii, lxxiii, lxxix, lxxxi, lxxxii, lxxxiii
General-in-Chief on Land and Sea	cxv

CONTENTS.

General-in-Chief of Van and Rear	lxxvi, lxxx
General-in-Chief of Cavalry	lxxxvi
General-in-Chief of Artillery	lxxv
General-in-Chief of Engineers ...	lxxxv
Chief of the Staff	lxxiv
Vanguard	xxxii
Crossing Rivers	xxxvi, xxxviii
Têtes-de-Pont	xxxix
Camps	xxii, xxxv, xciv
Tents and Bivouacs	lxii
Cantonments	... xxiv, lv
Field Fortifications	ciii
Line of Defence	... cxiii
Retreats ...	... vi, xv
Strong Places	xl
Sieges	xliii
Lines of Circumvallation	xlii, xliii, xcviii
Defence of Places	xliv, xlv, xcvi
Capitulations of Places of War	xlv, xlvi
Capitulations on the Battle-field	lxvii, lxix, c
The Three Arms ...	xlvii
Infantry	xlviii, xciii
Cavalry	l, li, lxviii, xci
Artillery ...	xcii

CONTENTS.

Infantry and Cavalry	xlix
Artillery and Infantry	... xciii
Artillery and Cavalry	lii
Artillery on March and in Position	liii, liv
Prisoners of War	lxiii, lxix, lxxxvii, cix
Conquered Provinces	... cx
Great Commanders	... lxxvii, lxxviii, cxii
Troops	lvi, cxi
Soldiers	... ... lviii, lix, lx
Speeches ...	... lxi
Praises of the Enemy	... cviii
A General a Traitor to his Country ...	... lxxi
Pillage	... cvii

II. ALPHABETICAL TABLE OF THOUGHTS.

Administration.
Affairs.
Agriculture.
Ambition.
Anarchy.
Architecture.
Aristocracy.
Armies.
Art of War.
Artillery.
Arts.
Audacity.
Authorities.
Advocates.

Bad Man.
Barkers of the Tribune.
Battle.
Battalions of Depôt.
Beggar.
Betray.
Body (Numerous).
Boldness.
Bravery.

Calculation.
Calumniate (to).
Cannon.
Cantata.

Character.
Charts.
Chief of State.
Chief (Military).
Civilization.
Circumstances.
Code of Safety.
Combats.
Command.
Commerce.
Congress.
Conquests.
Conscription.
Constancy.
Constitution.
Court.
Courage.
Courtiers.
Crimes.
Criminals.
Cynicism.
Church.
Coolness.
Civil War.
Chance.
Conquerors.
Conquered.
Custom.

ALPHABETICAL TABLE OF THOUGHTS.

Debasement.
Demeanour.
Declaimers.
Declamations.
Decorations.
Defence of Rivers and Lines.
Defensive.
Democracy.
Dishonour.
Disorder.
Despotism.
Drawing.
Dexterity.
Devotion to one's Country.
Dictatorship.
Discipline.
Dissipation.
Domination.
Divine Right.
Death.
Dogmatism.

English (the).
End (An).
Eye (A quick).
Edicts (Old).
Education.
Equality.
Equality of Taxation.
Energy.
Enemy.
Enthusiasm.
Enthusiasts.
Enterprises.
Epaulette.
Equilibrium (Political).

Esteem (Public).
Events.
Experience.
Evil.
Evil (Moral).
Eat.

Friends.
Faction.
Fanaticism.
Fanaticism (Military).
Favour (Popular).
Favourites of King.
Fashion.
Finances.
Flattery.
Flatterers.
Folly.
Force.
Force (Military).
Force (National).
Fortresses.
Fortune.
Freedom of Conscience.
French.
French Nation.
Fool.
Freedom (Political).
Future.

Good Sense.
Great Captain.
Garrisons.
General.
Glory.
Governors (Executive).
    See Rulers.

Alphabetical Table of Thoughts. xxi

Genius.
Gentleness.
God.
Government.
    ,,   Absolute.
    ,,   Free.
    ,,   Responsible.
Governed (the).
Ground.
Good People.
Great.
Grief.

Halt (to).
Happiness.
    ,,   Social.
Half Measures.
Herd (the).
Household (regulated).
Human Mind.
Human Weakness.
House (paternal).
Hatred.
Head.
Heroism.
Honour.
Honours.
Humour (bad).

Idealities.
Ideas.
Ignorance.
Imagination.
Immorality.
Indecision.
Industry.

Institutions.
Insulters.
Intelligence (superior).
Interest.
Intrigue.
Inventions.

Jealousy.
Judgment.
Judges.
Jury.
Just.
Justice.

Knowledge.
Kings.

Life.
  ,, Inner.
  ,, Private.
Love.
  ,, of Country.
Laurels.
Legislature
Legitimacy.
Line of Operation.
  ,, ,, Communication.
Logic.
Law (natural).
Laws.
  ,, Extraordinary.
Lies.
London.
Lawyers.

Make up one's mind (to).
Military Crimes.

Madness.
Mind.
Man.
,, Capable.
,, Good.
,, States.
,, Superior.
,, Honourable.
Misfortune.
Magistrates.
Manœuvre.
Martyrs.
Masses.
Master in his own house.
Mathematics.
Mistrust.
Memory.
Merit.
Method.
Minister of Religion.
Misery.
Moderation.
Moment Lost.
Monarchy.
Morale.
Morals.
Morality (public).
Means.
Multitude.
Music.

Name.
Nation.
,, French.
Nationality.
Necessity.

Neutrality
Nobility.

Observation.
Odious.
Offensive.
Officers.
Oligarchies.
Opinion.
,, Public.
Oppression.
Orators (political).
Order.
,, of Chivalry.
,, Material.
,, Moral.
,, Public.
,, Social.
One's Country.
Old Men.

Popularity (to lose).
People.
Printing.
Paradise.
Pardon.
Parties.
Passion.
Poor Man.
Pedant.
Persecution.
Perversity.
People (French).
,, Free.
,, Conquered.
Philosophy.

ALPHABETICAL TABLE OF THOUGHTS.

Point of Honour.
Police.
Political.
Pomp.
Position.
Power.
  ,, Absolute.
  ,, Political.
Prejudices.
Prerogatives.
Priests.
Princes.
Professions.
Prudence.

Qualities (military).

Rights of People.
Republic.
Republican Despotism.
Reason.
  ,, Political.
Reasoning.
Religious.
Religion.
Reinforcements.
Reputation.
Responsibilities.
Result.
Retreat.
Revenue.
Revolts.
Revolutions.
Rewards.
  ,, Social.
Ridicule.

Ribbons.
Rashness.
Rulers (see Governors).
Robber.

Silver.
Soul.
Strong Mind.
States.
  ,, Constitutional.
Soldiers.
Sciences.
Seditions.
Severity.
Simplicity.
Society.
Sovereign.
Sovereignty.
Sublime.
Success.
Suicide.
System (political).

Tactics.
Talents.
  ,, Warlike.
Time.
Terror.
Theology.
Tolerations.
Taxes.
Treatment (good).
Trappistiners.
Throne.
Troubles.
Tyranny.

Towns (commercial).

Unction (sacred).
Unfortunate.
Unity.

Vessel.
Valet de chambre.
Value.
Vengeance.
   ,, Popular.
Vices.
Victories.

Virtues.

War (art of).
Weakness.
War.
  ,, Mountain.
  ,, Siege.
World.
Wealth.
  ,, of States.
Work.

INTRODUCTORY LETTER.*

To
    His Royal Highness The Duke of
        Clarence and Avondale, K.G.,
                10th Royal Hussars.

Your Royal Highness,

General de Miribel, the present Head of the General Staff in France, describes in a few words the part that the Staff of an Army must now-a-days play:—" Though the Art of War may still hold in reserve for some future Turenne, or Condé, or Napoléon, those sudden inspirations of warlike genius—those lightning flashes that suddenly light up the tangled hosts and strike the foe at the very point needed to decide the fight,—yet, there is in the case of actual warfare a task to be done of a totally different kind. I am referring to

---

* We have nothing to add to this letter written long before the death of H.R.H. The Duke of Clarence. In this age of luxury and riches, it may seem to very few that there could be a moral, wise and beautiful, or good lesson, in so sudden a death of England's Royal Prince. At any rate, it did speak to our own mind, to us whose good and true friend His Royal Highness was When Bunyan's Pilgrim is in the House Beautiful, he prays that he may still remain poor ; we, all of us, in our sober moments, feel some doubt about the genuineness of happy Princes and Princesses; certainly there is the gloom as well as the glory of the Palace. And all we could do, with whole sympathy, was to say about England's Royal Family standing by the grave of the Royal Departed : *Et nunc, Reges, intelligite. Erudimini, qui judicatis terram!* Perhaps we may hope, though not with full confidence, that Death has proved to the Royal Soul, gone into Eternity, the relief from the shadowy splendour of the Throne of England's Queen for the happy security of God's Empire, within the confines of which there is only abiding content.—" I think we can hardly wish anything better for those we love than to be at rest in the World of Light."
—(*Cardinal Manning.*) L. E. HENRY.

the preparation for war, the preparatory work of bringing into the field those huge forces that the nation will one day be called upon to set in motion. I am referring to that patient, earnest, ceaseless work that devolves upon the Staff of an Army.

"Have you ever really thought upon the tedious and never-ceasing work that preparation for war implies now-a-days?

"Picture to yourselves then the stupendous armament of a whole nation; the sudden suspension of all public and private *life*; the transformation of France into one great drill-ground; the vast masses of men who must be clothed, equipped and armed in a few days, aye, in a few hours. Picture them speeding along by every railway to the confined spot where in one fearful encounter will be decreed the freedom, nay, the very existence of our Country.

"More than two millions of warriors, forming thousands of marching columns, or filling thousands of trains, will have to move on stated dates and at stated hours, following each other, crossing each other, halting at precise moments, and in pre-determined spots where all they need is to be found.

"All these human waves will appear to roll onward pell-mell; but at the given place and exact minute all will be found in order, each unit in its place, face to face with the foe, and ready for the struggle. And what a struggle!

"You do not imagine that when once those immense masses have been got together they can be moved or supplied or fed, or that they can take the field unless all the problems have been thought out and studied, and, so to speak, solved beforehand.

Introductory Letter. 3

"At such an hour it will not be in leisure and calm, but amid stress and tumult that the most difficult problems will have to be worked out and solved."*

What previous work and study, what strength of character must all this demand! This is the task before the staff of our modern armies. This is the work in all its pretentious vastness which I have but touched upon in outline and no more. General de Miribel's words are fit and timely, as we look at the future and what there is in store for soldiers.

Considering the recent crises and the present situation in England the British Public hardly yet realises that during the last three years England has given up the game in Asia; that the negociations with Russia amount to a retreat in the Far East; and that the Conference at the Hague, as Mr. Krausse clearly sees and shows in his book *Russia in Asia*, was in reality only an effort by her wiles and stratagems to hoodwink and to disarm England before the next Asiatic crisis, when England will either have to run away in Central Asia, as she has done in North China, or to fight Russia on terms infinitely less favourable than at present.† Fighting

---

* It has been shown, on inquiry, that there are 5,250,000 soldiers on a *permanent* war footing about the world at present. There would be 44,250,000 men under the colours in the event of a general conflict. If these armed men got the order to kill the rest of the world's inhabitants, each man could only kill his 32 persons, and not one more. The next thing to be their own mutual extermination between soldiers and soldiers; and thus would come off, of course, the whole and final end of man's kind.

All the soldiers in the world set in one row would make quite a tight rope round the equator. One single musketry discharge from their rifles would cost over £1,000,000. To review them would take seventy days to a train going at full speed and without one stop. (L. E. H.)

† Are not Russia and England at loggerheads about securing substantial acquisitions from Persia? Russia, on her side, is trying hard to secure for her own trade the sea outlets of the Persian Gulf. England, on the other side, needs the co-operation of Persia in order to be permitted to establish her railway communications between Asia, Africa, and India. (L. E. H.)

must take place in Europe before long again ; human appetite and passion by no means get easier to tame as we are nearing the XXth Century than at the time of David and Uriah, of rich Ahab and poor Naboth. Gold "kidnaps" the Bath-she-Bas and the Jezebels as cheerfully on this day as in the days of Nathan and Elijah. I now forget who said : *The best of men can never live at peace If 'tis not pleasing to his wicked neighbour.* The relaxation of tension in the relations between Central European powers, England with them, is temporary. Between the six leading Nations in the Christian world—Austria, England, France, Germany, Italy, and Russia ; and China, Japan, and the United States far away from us—are relations cordial and sound *truly* ? Or are they not *neutrally* patient perforce, and silently maintaining and accepting this durance with dignity ; but anticipating rather the unavoidable liquidation on one early day of International contentions by the customary means of War. Russia is waiting till after the completion of the Siberian Railway to fling out the glove of challenge. In my opinion a great European war is in the wind. *Væ victis!* Even smaller States keep unceasingly at the work of strengthening their national defences. As if to illustrate the usefulness of Napoléon's teaching as contained in this book, fortifications are being built round Sofia, and the Capital is getting converted into a fortified camp ; military works are extended from Slivinitza to Sofia, and communications improved with Shumla, Rustchuck and Slivno. Englishmen may feel certain that whenever they find themselves involved in a great war, hostilities will have been sprung suddenly on England, when England's foes—France, Germany, or Russia, may be the three together—have made every preparation and deem her at their mercy. History records innumerable instances where fighting has occurred long before any formal declaration of war. (Read with attention the simple and skilfully got up Abstract of the cases of *Hostilities without declaration of War, from 1700 to 1870*, by Colonel J. F. MAURICE, R.A., P.S.C., Professor of Military History at the Staff College.) To mention nothing else, the Mediterranean and the St. Lawrence can both tell their tale on that point. Again: Socialistico-Democratic masses are becoming more self-assured and turbulent: the bugbear of revolution and republicanism keeps more than one prince in a troubled state of mind. Again: many statesmen, who shrink from the dangers that threaten them, sacrifice their conscience and their oath to the menaces of the mob, growing tumultuous and ungovernable, in England even. The Charter given to the School Board was not to educate the poor who live by labouring, for a higher sphere of life, as it does— thereby giving a death blow to an essential and vital element of Society—but for the sphere they are in, and in which they earn their livelihood. In its teaching it has totally lost sight of that. The great progress made in the technical and mechanical arts which contribute to the benefits of life is mainly due to individual ingenuity and the workshop—not to any school teaching. Hand-labour is by Divine right the poor man's inheritance; but his *duty* is to work with his hands. As a Christian as well as a Prime Minister Lord Salisbury must, therefore, be *against* secular education. The increasing contempt for public order by the masses, indeed, is a sign of the times and a serious factor of danger to the State, from which sober men, who know the populace, draw their own conclusions as to the fall or death of princes. In these times of emphatic peace-preaching *versus* swelling ruffianism, force alone, as in the stirring days of Chartism, can keep down petty rivalries and approaching revolution. Napoléon made the practical discovery that "though nations may be conquered by the sword, they cannot be governed by the sword without religion." In that conclusion he had his great rival contemporary the Duke of Wellington with him : "Men educated without religion will only be clever devils."—(*Speech in the House of Lords.*)

Princes are powerless to get power back lost once in surrendering conscience for the sake of ambition and gain. In Rome—the capital of Christendom—the disgusting scenes of violence and fighting, caused by the Socialists and Republicans in the Italian Parliament, are an object lesson to the point. The one answer to disorderly aggressiveness of Revolution and Socialistico - Democratic strike rioting, whether at Brussels or Toronto, Paris or Tunbridge Wells and Clapham Common, is and must be always — *Fix bayonets!* (*Gallicè :* Grenadiers, *en avant!*) This is THE ONLY WAY to defend honest masters and workers against all cliques of unscrupulous Socialists and dense "demagogues"("vessels filled with beer or other liquors," according to Mark Twain). Discipline and Republicanism or Socialism are two opposing forces which cannot be brought together. The political system of Royalty does not make a man a discontented Radical, but, on the contrary, a staunch upholder of authority and order ; simple Christians, upright people, and of good faith, the bulk of French Royalists are. The Republican system is precisely the reverse. The reason is not far to seek, and is too important, as bearing on the whole national peace and happiness, to be passed over.

Royalist leaders are social gentlemen; Republicans, as a class, are not. I disdain all intention of entering into exposition of invidious comparisons. But— *parva componere magnis* — place Englishmen and Americans side by side. I am speaking of patent facts under our eyes, as warranted from the unceasing American Immigration into England. They are sufficient, because they give us principles and warnings to govern our conduct. If now and then Noblemen seem helpless to resist the claims of the Lower Orders, made by paid agitators discontented and unreliable, it is through the clumsy arrogance and disdain of a few aristocratic blackguards or *blancs-becs*, who will never set the Thames on fire, because they have not even the honest enthusiasm, the frankness and courage, of Sir Francis Burdett.

Disagreement, contention, and fighting there must exist so long as there live one Adam with one Eve to offend on this world of ours, and so long as there are to be found brewers and distillers to fill the bottle. We are members of Humanity as a body—and is not Humanity damned rascality?

At this time of the near end of the fast disappearing nineteenth century, Europe, worse off than in 1848, stands visibly honeycombed with Revolutionary Societies composed of ugly customers who lie in ambush for National and International commotions, and for the money of Plutocrats before everything else. Take the effervescent and volatile France, where the masses are still struggling for political and social freedom after a third trial, thirty years old, of Republican Government. Spain, the land of the Cid, rent and torn by civil strife. Italy, where the king lives in terror of his life, a bankrupt country and in a deplorable state of disorganization. Belgium, one of the freest Continental countries, where the king, in open conflicts with factory-hands and miners, is safe upon his throne no longer, nor is Monarchy likely to hold its ground. Austria, with her sincere and great love for her venerable Emperor Francis Joseph, tottering like a reed under the uncheckable growth of virulent anti-semitism in Vienna and Budapest. The stolid and staid Prussia, the martinet nation of the Continent, internally perturbed by socialism and by agrarian restlessness. As to Russia—the Colossus of the North—the Rev. Philip Young puts the suggested questions in the *United Service Magazine*: " For what purpose are Russia's immense armaments maintained? For self protection? Assuredly not. No nation has any desire to attack the Great Northern Power. Invasion would be futile. One retreat from Moscow suffices for the world's military history." He comes to the conclusion that Great Britain, at all events, cannot afford to dispense with a single soldier or sailor, however sympathetically she may view the scheme outlined in the Czar's proposals. Here the Rev. Philip Young is not in accord with Major-General Bengough, who expresses the opinion in the same Magazine, *The Ethics of War*, that the establishment of the principle of arbitration on a solid and workable basis seems likely to be the one practical outcome of the labours of the Peace Convention.* Even

---

* In connection with the recently-met Peace Conference at the Hague, it is of interest to bear in mind that during the Seven Years' War (1756—1763) it had been proposed to form a European Court of Arbitration. But it is still more interesting to remember what Frederick the Great thought and did with regard to that proposal. It was on 28th July, in 1758. The King of Prussia put aside this question of an International Court of Arbitration between France, England, Sweden, and Russia, and wrote:—" If the French, Austrians, and Russians have anything to say, let them speak out. But as far as I am concerned, I shall confine myself to defeating them and being silent." Instead of 1758 put 1899, and remember that Europe is none the more ready to make peace to-day than it was then. (I., E. II.)

in *insouciante* England, unfortunately, an alliance between Plutocracy has taken place and the proletarian Electorate which is bent on putting down "Squiredom and Parsondom"; and which will end its career, as it did in France, in putting down the Queen and all organized order. For its strong-minded masses, while still contending for more political privileges, though spoilt by endless grants of larger social advantages, are leavened with the spirit of weak agnosticism and weedy socialism.* Who or what else but the sword can protect abiding order against popular anarchy, or quell international outbreaks which may arise and require the necessary intervention of armed forces in places where high moral and religious principles, combined with reason, fail, and are reduced to absolute powerlessness? The *Deum timeto* and *Regem honorato*, as commanded by the Bible, seems false piety to many men now-a-days, whose sole fear is that of the policeman, of the cat-o'-nine tails, and Jack Ketch.†

Yes, in the grave national and international problems that have to be dealt with now, Europe stands harder pressed to-day than in 1848. Western Christendom is

* Did not Lord Kitchener say at the ATBARA BRIDGE OPENING on August 26th, 1899, when congratulating the American foremen and workmen on the excellent success which has crowned their efforts in the erection of this bridge in the heart of Africa, far from their homes during the hottest months of the year, and depending solely on the labour of men speaking a foreign tongue :— "I think it demonstrates that the relations between Labour and Capital in our Country"—English firms found it impossible to take up the order for the bridge—"are not such as to give sufficient confidence to Capitalists to induce them to run the risk of establishing great up-to-date workshops, with the plant necessary to enable Great Britain to maintain her proud position as the first constructing Nation of the world."—And Lord Kitchener, the ardent friend of France and tried on the battlefields of the 1870-71 War, is not the soldier made from an inflammable stuff. (L. E. H.)

† *Vide* the Book "Conséquences de l'établissement du Suffrage universel en France." By L. MARIOTTE.

not yet, nay, it can *never* become free from the alarming obligations which are the true outcome of the current increase in military and naval armaments over our known world; from North Cape of Norway to Cape Matapan in Greece, and from Cape La Roca to Cape Apsheron, without naming the crowding and tangled Foreign Questions of Asiatic, African and American growth.

The Peace Conference at The Hague has been struggling exhausted, and good for not much against this scandalous waste and mis-spending of national money by the governing class in war-like preparations. These schemes and provisions offer thrilling and appetising visions to the fighting man individually no doubt. Nevertheless, current armaments stand as a crying shame and sin against our so-named European *civilization* or *progressiveness*. After all said, the boasted progressiveness of Western Christendom is but a sparkling word first used by certain agnostic or fashionable worldlings to cloak their dark ambitions. And, in the next place, it is a term palatable—just the right one— the least likely to sadden and to discourage credulous believers in the proteiform Christianity of Foreign and Colonial Offices in Europe—a Christianity manifestly a bottomless sham; and, indeed, not the Christianity of the Prince of Peace.

Lasting unity and harmony between nations, as between individuals, are but a fallacy, like the Reunion of Christendom and Arbitration. To what heaps of cowardly deeds is not man's life an answer? Look round and observe the *Moral Cowards* and the *Bombastes Furioso* (also called *Gas-Bag* at Dover) of Contemporary Society! Though Sibylline a bit, I am not a petty and self-interested faddist; but I say that war alone, therefore, must settle the threatening dangers from within as from without.

As a soldier, and as a leader of men, General de

Introductory Letter.

Miribel had been tried under the crucial test of "fire" again and again on the battlefields of the Crimea, Italy, and Mexico; and finally, in the war of 1870-71, when they saw him fighting like a lion and pointing the guns at Buzenval, Champigny, and Le Bourget. His good name and popularity throughout the French army were worth knowing; they said of him that he was, before all others, the one *sur qui l'on compte*. He was a chief whose heart was in his work; being a general whose success contrasted so strongly with the sad records of his predecessors in the same office. In the face of a conceited and over ill-advised belief of the French in their invincibility, as preached to them by miscreants controlling French opinion and by so-called politicians, whose patriotism is not superior to party interest, he unhesitatingly accepted and acknowledged the innate superiority of the army—superiority by venal Pressmen denied the limits of strict truth in England—and set to work. He kept clear of political shoals and of the unrelenting plague and great calamity of division, which in France wreck so many useful men.* Thereby General de Miribel was giving his army and his countrymen the impression that he had qualities to alarm jealousy, and excellence to deserve trust in future events; his wisdom was unquestioned and his foresight seasonable. His death was truly a national loss and an eventful calamity.†

* Since the fall of the Empire, beginning with M. Jules Favre, the queerly motley de-Galliffet-cum-Millerand Administration is the THIRTY-NINTH Ministry of the Third Republic!—The fickleness of common lovers! (L. E. H.)

† Well remembered is the name of General de Miribel, now dead, and rightly succeeded at the head of the French Army by his disciple and friend, General Le Mouton de Boisdeffre. While out for a ride in his meadows, close to his country house—Château du Châtelard (Drôme)—on September 11, 1893, he was thrown from his horse, was picked up unconscious, and died insensible. He was 62 years old. To us, the one nearest and dearest to the heart of the late General de Miribel, wrote on the occasion of her husband's terrible death: "*Il fut passionné pour le bien et pour le devoir. J'ai la confiance que cette âme si droite a été récompensée et qu'elle prie pour son Pays et pour ceux qu'il a aimés.*" Certainly this touching reference to this grand Frenchman and Soldier by his sorrowing widow was truth. (L. E. H.)

All the problems for the field of battle have to be thought out, and, so to speak, solved beforehand.

In time of peace a future commander of soldiers thus should closely study the records of past fighting, and struggles of modern generals; the great conqueror, and chief of the warriors of the Grand Army, has taught lessons so practical and ever so worthy of study that, fatal to the pride of France as the Star of the Napoléons has proved, the genius of Napoléon the Great cannot be admired too much, and his mind too closely studied as a General, and even in Republican France, the name of the Great Emperor still retains a powerful hold over the popular mind. Alone, Marshal Von Moltke's words will put an end once for all to equivocal teaching:—'Whoever is well enough acquainted with the Campaigns of Napoléon, and familiar enough with them to be able to recall at any moment, the details of his battles, and the movements that he ordered, has always in his hand the key to the movements proper to make under any given circumstance whatever.' The book published to-day contains Napoléon's mind; and our purpose is to make Napoléon's genius more and more familiarly known to students of the soldier's science. Officers of all ranks in the Queen's Army, and particularly future staff officers, may care to think over these Military Maxims and Thoughts of the greatest soldier of this soon waning century. The object of this book is to assist such officers in acquiring an amount of knowledge expected from any military man fairly intelligent. It may also be useful in saving the trouble of referring to information, scattered, and often not easily obtainable from books.

In his observations on military affairs, General Monk, Duke of Albemarle, says:—'Reading and discourse

Introductory Letter. 13

are requisite to make a soldier perfect in the military art, however great his practical knowledge may be.' These particular war truths are—General Burnod (late in the service of Russia) says—the mind of the greatest and most wonderful commander of armies in modern times and of his masterly manœuvres and operations in the field. Military art is learnt by a careful, thorough and constant study of the numerous campaigns of Gustavus Adolphus, Turenne, and Condé, and of more recent date of Frederick-the-Great, and Wellington; but chiefly of the stupendous military operations of Bonaparte—a not unworthy rival of Alexander the Great and the Carthaginian Hannibal, in whom the revolutionary spirit was embodied, politically and militarily. Such principles appear to me likely to guide all eminent generals; indeed, more than once of late years, during the great American War and the Franco-German War, our attention has been drawn to this highly serviceable and classical teaching from Napoléon's War Thoughts and Maxims, as illustrated through the great encounters of the heroic Grant, Lee, Sherman, and Von Moltke, against their respective foes. Consequently it must be by comparing such valuable records of military history that present and future commanders of armies can, while preparing the plans of their own campaigns, realize the prospective wisdom of Napoléon's marvellous work in the field, and then apply it effectually, according to exigencies that may arise, and in a practical shape; and each commander, according to his own country and genius, will force his way through the thorns and thickets of that gloomy labyrinth of war.

I had thought at first that I could strictly adhere to collating together Napoléon's miscellaneous axioms as maxims, but when I noticed the shortness of the book I have tried to make up for its deficiencies by perusing the memoirs of the venerated and esteemed Montecuculli, and the general orders to his commanders of the Great Frederick, King of Prussia. The similarity between their precepts and Napoléon's convinced me that the science of war is open to study under two distinct heads. The one consists in taking into account the genius and knowledge of the commander entirely ; and the other lies in taking up and dissecting the working points or details only. The former mode of study remains the same at all times and for all countries, and whatever be the fighting weapons and engines ; in which case identical war rules have guided great Generals, no doubt, of every age ; the working points or details, on the contrary, remain subject to changes, and discoveries, and temper of nations, and improved weapons, which influence all and are most active.

In view of showing the correctness of my ideas and reasoning, I give facts selected from various times and campaigns illustrating these maxims ; and I also wish to prove that there should not be, because there cannot be, anything *problematical*—I mean lucky and unlucky *by chance**—in the science of war, but that defeat and victory depend always, or nearly always, on the genius and acquired knowledge and various endowments of the commander of an army in the field.

Napoléon's Social and Political Thoughts contain great and useful lessons too. They show how deep a knowledge of men, their passions, faults and weaknesses, this great soldier and reformer possessed to attain to the height of power where he would have remained but for the treason of a small number of men whom he had

---

* Some there be who may not agree at all with me and who contend that the thing is to recognise and avail yourself of *chance*. Chance is the exception to our general rule. "*Ne obliviscaris.*" (L. E. H.)

overwhelmed with riches and honours. The soldiers who read this book to advantage, and think over the brilliant campaigns in Italy and under the Empire, will see how worthy they all are of the renown of Napoléon, and beyond all comparison. From it they will draw true rules of art in war, and inform themselves by the study of the finest operations that have ever been carried out. They will admire the great deeds of that Imperial Army which has not ceased to be National, to be France herself in reality, and which has been sufficiently proved by its sublime devotion in 1814-15 when its opponents were meditating, preaching and intriguing for the betrayal of their Country ; of that army which, after having thrown into shade by its exploits and wonders—the very wonders of Ancient Heroes—has given both to the present and future generations an example of the finest Patriotism by disbanding with incomparable calmness and dignity, when so many brave Frenchmen gave up for the repose of their agonizing country their chances of revenge, the future prospects of an honoured career, those honourably proved arms so long the terror of the foe, and finally their personal safety.

By this noble resignation, the brave soldiers of the Republic and the Empire, who have preserved to this day the love of France and of Heroic Deeds in the mind and love of their grandsons, showed their foes, whether at home or abroad, that they had always looked upon Napoléon as the head and the representative of Military France and Frenchmen, because there had ever been found in Napoléon the warmest patriotism and affection for France. *Ses paroles sont des oracles, son souvenir remplit le monde, et son nom est la plus grande gloire de la France !*

I have the honour of being a soldier's son and the grandson of a French Commander* who fought and was "under fire" in twenty-one campaigns under Napoléon from Russia to Italy, and Spain and Germany to Boulogne, who was twice wounded on the battlefield (once whilst fighting the English at Vittoria), who was knighted twice—once by Napoléon and once by King Louis XVIII. I do not hesitate in concluding with General Husson's quotation of the true and fine words of the Duke of Vicenza: "The memory of Napoléon will always bring forth heroes, inspire in young men that noble ambition and emulation which produces great citizens. His exploits will be repeated in far off ages; and wherever a French heart is, it will inscribe on his banner: 'Honour and admiration to the memory of Napoléon as a Soldier!'"

With these explanations, and with grateful acknowledgment of the high honour conferred on me by Your Royal Highness, in graciously accepting my dedication, I leave my work to the discernment of the Army and Officers whose kind encouragement is supporting me through my labours.

I have the honour to be most respectfully
Your Royal Highness's
Grateful and obedient servant,

LUCIEN HENRY

(Ex-1ᵉʳ Régiment de Zouaves)

Professor.

Staff College, July, 1889.

---

* *M. Philippe Henry, de Verdun (Lorraine), Officier Supérieur commandant le 55e Régiment d'Infanterie de Ligne et les Légions Actives de la Marne.*

PART I.

WAR MAXIMS.

BOOK I.

I.

The Frontiers of States are either great rivers or chains of mountains, or a desert. Of all these obstacles opposing the progress of an army, the most difficult to surmount is the desert, next comes the mountains, and third only, the large rivers.

II.

A plan of campaign ought to have foreseen what the enemy is able to do, and should contain the means of checkmating him. Such plans are liable to endless modification, according to the circumstances, the genius of the commander, the kind of troops, and the topography of the seat of war, and weather.

III.

An army marching to the conquest of a country has its two wings flanked by neutral ground or by great natural obstacles, such as rivers or chains of mountains ; it may happen that only one of its wings is so supported, or even that both wings are exposed. In the first case the general in command has only to guard his centre from being forced ; in second, he must bear on the supported wing ; in third, he must have his troops bearing well on his centre, and they must never separate ; for if it is a difficulty to have two flanks in confusion, this is doubled when there are four, and it is tripled when there are six, *i.e.*, when the army is divided into two or three different corps. The line of operation in the first case may bear indifferently on the left or right; in the second case it must bear on the supported wing; and in the third case it should be perpendicular to the middle of the army's line of march. But in all the cases abovementioned, after every five or six days of marching, works should be erected, or an entrenchment thrown up along the line of operations, to serve as a depôt for provisions and arms, as an organising station for convoys or columns, and as a centre of movement, and as a guiding mark, to shorten the line of operation of the army.

IV.

When one marches to the conquest of a country with two or three armies, each having its line of operation, but all to meet at a fixed point, it is a principle that the junction of these several corps should never be effected in the vicinity of the foe, for not only could the enemy by concentrating, prevent this junction, but may beat them in detail also.

V.

All war should be methodical, for every war should have an aim, and be constructed in accordance with the principles and rules of art. It should be carried on with means proportional to the obstacles which can be foreseen.

VI.

At the commencement of a campaign thought should be expended as to whether an advance should be made or not, but when once the offensive has been assumed it should be maintained to the last extremity. Whatever skill may be shown in manœuvres in a retreat, it will always weaken the *moral* of the army, since by giving up the chances of success, they are given over to the foe. Retreats, besides, cost more in men and war material than the bloodiest fights, since in a battle the enemy loses as well as you do, while in a retreat you lose and he does not.

VII.

An army should always, night and day, and in any hour, be prepared to offer all the resistance of which it is capable; and this demands that the troops should constantly have with them their arms and ammunition, the infantry with its artillery, cavalry and generals; that the different divisions of the army should be constantly in a position to support, sustain, and protect one another; that whether in camp, on the march, or at the halt, the troops should be always in a position of vantage, which has the qualities necessary for every battle-field, *i.e.*, that the flanks should be well supported, and that all weapons should be placed in the most advantageous position to be brought into immediate play.

When the army is *en route* there should always be scouts in front and to the right and left, to give information, and placed at such a distance, that the main body of the army may deploy and take up its position unmolested.*

---

* The Dreyfus case has shown that the spy system is indissolubly bound up with an army's Intelligence Department in peace time. How much more it is inseparable from it to supply the commander with information when on the field of operations we need not insist upon. In Canning's " Life and Times " by the late Mr. H. G. Stapleton, p. 125, I read how within one of the folds of the very tent in which Napoléon and Alexander were discussing the fate of the nations on the 25th June, 1807, there was all the time hidden a listener who lost no time in communicating to the English Government the agreement come to between the two Emperors to divide the world. All the time the two Potentates had believed themselves personally and absolutely alone on their own raft; the other raft was reserved for the most confidential members of their

VIII.

A general-in-chief should say to himself during the day: "If the enemy's army were to appear on my front, or on my right or on my left, what would I do?" And if he finds the question hard to answer, he is not properly posted, things are not well ordered, and he must put matters right, and at once.

IX.

The strength of an army, like the quantity of motion in mechanics, is estimated by the mass multiplied by the velocity. A swift march enhances the *moral* of the army and increases its power for victory.

X.

With an army inferior in number, cavalry or artillery—it would be well to avoid a general engagement, to supply the defect in number by rapid marches, the want of artillery by manœuvres, and the inferiority in cavalry by the choice of a good position. In such a position the *moral* of a soldier counts for much.

XI.

To operate in directions far from one another and without communication is a fault which usually leads to the commission of another. The detached column has orders but for the first day; for the next, its operations depend upon what has happened to the principal column; thus, according to circumstances, this column will lose

---

personal staff. The report to Canning was a direct one consequently from the very tent of the two Emperors. So much for police and spying work. But the spy—this hell-born man or woman causing such havoc in once happy homes—is a dangerous tool to use, and only to be treated with ignominy. An officer dealing with a spy—whose preying on his fellows produces such dire results as we have read of in the above case—cannot be too watchful, and he should remain a *gentleman*, while never missing an opportunity when at least it is granted him fairly. Belgians and Italians are said to make the most serviceable and ready spies. (L. E. H.)

time in waiting for orders, or more likely it will act at random. It ought to be then a principle that an army should have all its columns together, so that the enemy could find no possible means of getting in between them. When, for any reasons whatever, this maxim is departed from, it is necessary that the detached bodies should be independent in their operations ; they should bear on to a fixed point where they are to assemble ; they should march without hesitation and without new orders ; finally, they should be as little as possible subject to isolated attack.

XII.

An army ought to have but one line of operation, which should be carefully preserved, and abandoned only as the result of weightier and overbearing considerations.

XIII.

The distance which should intervene between the divisions of an army in the marches depends on the locality, the circumstances, and the aim in view.

XIV.

In mountains, there are everywhere a large number of positions extremely strong in themselves, which one should take care not to attack. The spirit of war lies in placing yourself either on the flanks, or on the rear of the foe, which would leave him no alternatives but to evacuate his position without fighting to take a new one in the rear, or to come on and attack you. In mountain warfare, the attack is under a disadvantage ; even in offensive war, art displays itself in having only defensive fights and in obliging the enemy to attack.

XV.

Glory and military honour is the first duty a general should consider when he is going to fight ; the safety and the preservation of his men is secondary; but this very boldness and tenacity ensures the safety and economy of life. In retreating, besides the honours of war, more men are often lost than in two battles; therefore, we should never despair, while brave men still remain with the colours, so we obtain—and deserve to obtain—victory.

XVI.

A well-tested maxim of war, is not to do what the enemy wishes simply because he does wish it; thus it is good to avoid the battle-field he has reconnoitred and studied, and still more should care be taken to avoid one he has fortified, or where he is entrenched. A consequence of this principle is never to attack a position in front, which may be taken by turning.

XVII.

In a war of marching and manœuvring, to avoid a battle against superior forces, it is necessary to entrench every night, and to occupy always a good position of defence. The position which nature usually furnishes cannot shelter an army against superior forces without the help of art.

XVIII.

Surprised* by a superior force, an ordinary general occupying a bad position would seek safety in retreat; but a good commander will put a bold face on it and march to meet the foe. By such action he disconcerts his opponent, and, if the latter shows any irresolution in his march, a skilful general, profiting by this moment of indecision, may even hope for victory, or at least gain the day by manœuvring; at night he can entrench himself

---

* One great maxim is, "A general may be defeated; he should never be *surprised.*" (L. E. H.)

or fall back on a better position. By such bold action he maintains the honour of war, that important essential in the strength of an army.

XIX.

The passage from defensive to offensive action is one of the most difficult operations in war.

XX.

We should not abandon our line of operations; but it is one of the most skilful manœuvres in the art of war to be able to change it when circumstances authorize it. An army which changes skilfully its line of operation deceives the foe, who no longer knows its rear and its weak points.

XXI.

When an army is followed by a siege-train, by wounded or invalids, it should not make its stages too long, in order to reach the depôts as soon as possible.

XXII.

The art of camping on a position is the same as the forming of a line of battle on this position. To do this, all arms should be favourably placed in order to be brought into action; we should choose a position which is not commanded and which cannot be turned; and, if it be possible, it should command and envelop the enemy's position.

XXIII.

When in a position where the enemy threatens to hem you in, it is necessary at once to mass one's forces, and threaten the enemy by an offensive move; by this manœuvre you prevent him from withdrawing troops to disturb your flanks, in case you should judge it imperative to beat a retreat.

XXIV.

One maxim of war, that ought never to be forgotten, is to place the cantonments at a point most distant and most sheltered from the enemy, especially when the latter is preparing a surprise. In this manner time will be gained to mass together the whole army before the enemy can attack.

XXV.

When two armies are fighting, and the one must, for retreat, proceed in but one direction, while the other may retire on all points of the compass, all the advantages rest with this latter. That is the time for a general to be bold, to strike hard blows and to manœuvre with effect on the hostile flanks: victory is in his hands.

XXVI.

It is acting against the truest principles to allow separate action to two divisions which have no communication with one another, in face of an army centralized, and with easy internal communication.

XXVII.

When one is driven from a first position, it is well to rally one's columns sufficiently to the rear to prevent the enemy interposing, for nothing could be more untoward for columns to be attacked separately before their junction.

XXVIII.

A detachment must not be made on the eve of battle, for in the night the situation may change—either by movements of the enemy towards retreat, or by the arrival of large reinforcements which allow it even to take the offensive—and render the premature dispositions made, futile.

XXIX.

When about to deliver battle, it is the general rule to concentrate all your forces, and to neglect none; one battalion often decides the day.

XXX.

Nothing is more rash and contrary to the principles of war than to make a flank march before an army in position, especially when this army occupies heights, below which it is necessary to defile.

XXXI.

Secure yourself all possible chances of success when you decide to deliver an important engagement, especially when you are dealing with a great general, for if you are beaten, and you are in the midst of your magazines, and close to your fortress, woe to the conquered!

XXXII.

The duty of a vanguard does not consist merely of advancing and falling back, but in manœuvring. It should be composed of light cavalry, supported by a reserve of cavalry of the line, and by battalions of infantry, also having batteries as supports. It is requisite that troops of the vanguard should be picked men, and that the generals, officers, and soldiers should be well up in their tactics, each according to the requirements of his grade. Troops not thus instructed would only offer embarrassment to the vanguard.

XXXIII.

It is contrary to the usages of war to let one's parks and heavier pieces of artillery enter a defile if the other end is not held also; in case of retreat they will be in the way and be lost. They should be left ready, and under a suitable escort until mastery is obtained of the outlet.

XXXIV.

It should be held as a maxim to have no intervals between the different bodies forming the line of battle, unless it be done to get the enemy into a trap.

XXXV.

The camps of an army should be so pitched as to be a protection to one another.

XXXVI.

When the hostile army is covered by a river on which there are several *têtes-de-pont* it is no use approaching in front, this would scatter your army and expose you to be cut off. You must come to the river with your columns echelonned, so that there should be but one column, *i.e.*, the one right in front, which the enemy could attack without risking his own flank. In the meantime the light troops will reach the banks of the river, and having fixed on the part where they wish to cross it, let them bear down on it rapidly, and throw the bridge; it should be observed that the place of crossing should be at some distance from the leading echelon, in order to deceive the enemy.

XXXVII.

As soon as one is master of a position commanding the opposite bank facilities are acquired for effecting the crossing of the stream, especially if this position is of sufficient extent to hold a large number of pieces of artillery.* This advantage is less when the stream is more than 600 yards wide, for, the grape shot not reaching the other side, the troops resisting the passage can easily march past and shelter themselves from fire. It would come to this: that the grenadiers who are ordered

---

* Present ranges of weapons, to which Regimental Officers could not possibly pay too great attention, alter all these conditions. (L. E. H.)

to cross the river, to protect the construction of the passage, might reach the other bank, but would then be crushed by the enemy's fire, since their batteries, placed at a distance of 400 yards from the outlet of the bridge, would be able to open a very murderous fire, and yet be more than 1,000 yards distant from the batteries of the army wishing to pass over; so that the whole advantage in artillery lies on their side. In this case, too, the passage is impossible, unless it be by a successful surprise, or through the protection of an intervening island, or by taking advantage of a very pronounced bend, which would permit the establishment of batteries crossing their fires on the gorge. This isle or bend forms then a natural *tête-de-pont*, and gives the advantage to the attacking army.

When a river is less than 120 yards broad, and a command is obtained of the opposite bank, the troops who have been landed on the other side, being under the protection of artillery, are so advantageously placed that, unless the river makes a bend, it is impossible for the enemy to prevent the establishment of the bridge. The bridge being a defile, a semi-circle should be formed about its extremity, and the army must march past the fire of the opposite sides at a distance of 600 or 800 yards.

XXXVIII.

It is difficult to prevent an enemy who has crossing apparatus from passing over a river. When the army which opposes the passage has, as its aim, to cover a siege, it should take steps to arrive before the enemy in a position intermediate between the river and the place to be covered as soon as the general commanding feels he cannot prevent the crossing.

XXXIX.

Turenne, in the campaign of 1645, was driven back with his army on Philipsburg by large forces; there was no bridge over the Rhine, but he took advantage of the ground between the bank and the Rhine as a suitable spot to be occupied. This should be a lesson to officers of talent, not only as to the construction of strong places, but also for that of *têtes-de-pont*. A space should be left between the place and the river, such that, without entering the place which would compromise its safety, an army might form and rally between the place and the bridge. An army retiring on Mayence, being pursued, is necessarily compromised, since more than one day is needed to pass over the bridge and the extent of Cassel is too small for an army to stay without encumbrance; there ought to have been 400 yards between the place and the Rhine. It is essential that the *têtes-de-pont* before large rivers should be traced after this principle, else they would offer but sorry help to the passage of a retreating army. The *têtes-de-pont* taught in schools are only good before small streams where the passage is not long.

XL.

Strong places are useful in offensive as in defensive war. They could not indeed stop the advance of an army, but they offer excellent means of delaying, checking, weakening, and harassing a victorious enemy.

XLI.

There are but two ways of effectually besieging a place, one by first defeating the hostile army entrusted with the duty of covering it and driving the remnants beyond some natural obstacle, *e.g.*, mountains, or a great river; the covering force being removed, an observing army must be placed behind the natural obstacle, until the siege-works are completed and the place taken. But if it is desired to take the place in face of a reinforcing army without the risk of a battle, one must be provided with a siege-train, with ammunition and provisions, for the expected duration of a siege, and lines of contravallation and circumvallation, taking advantage of localities such as heights, woods, marshes, inundations. There being no need to maintain communication with the depôt posts, there is only need to keep the relieving army in check; in this case an observing army should be formed to keep an eye on the relief force, and bar its way to the place, by means of which it is always possible to attack it in the flank or rear if it attempts to steal a march; by taking advantage of the lines of circumvallation, a part of the besieging might be employed to deliver battle to the relieving army. Thus, to besiege a place before a hostile army, you must cover the siege by lines of circumvallation. If the army is strong enough, after having left before the place a body four times the garrison, to number yet an equal figure with the army of relief, it may be more than one march distant; if after this detachment it be inferior in number, it should be but a short march from the siege, in order to be able to fall back on its lines, or rather, to receive reinforcements in case of attack. If the two armies engaged in the siege and in observation together are but equal to the relieving force, the whole of the besieging army should remain in or near the lines, and confine itself to pushing forward the siege operations with all the vigour possible.

XLII.

Feuquières has said you are never to wait for the enemy within the lines of circumvallation; but sally out and attack him. Feuquières is wrong; there is no dogmatic rule in war, nor should there be one against waiting for the foe within the lines.*

XLIII.

Those who would reject lines of circumvallation and all the assistance the engineers' art can afford, deprive themselves gratuitously of an aid which is never hurtful, almost always useful, and often indispensable. However, the principles of field fortification have made no progress since the time of the ancients; it is even below what it was 2,000 years ago. Encouragement then should be given to officers of talent to perfect this part of their art, and to bring it to the same level with the others.

XLIV.

Circumstances not permitting that a sufficiently large garrison should be left behind to defend a fortress containing hospital and stores, all measures should be taken to secure the citadel from being stormed.

XLV.

A fortified place cannot protect the garrison and keep off the enemy but for a certain time; when this has expired, the garrison must lay down its arms. All civilized people are agreed on this point, and the only controversy has been as to the length of the defence a governor should make before capitulating. However, some generals, among them Villars, think a governor should never surrender; but when at the last extremity, he is to blow up the fortifications and profit by the confusion to cut his way through the besieging force. When this is not possible, they can always march out with the garrison and save the men.†

---

* This should cut both ways though.

† This was done at Verdun during the 1870-71 War and *avec les honneurs de la guerre*. (L. E. H.)

Commanders who have adopted this plan have rejoined their army with three-fourths of their garrison.

XLVI.

The keys of a fortified place are well worth the liberty of its garrison, when the latter is resolved not to leave it except as free men; thus it is always more advantageous to grant an honourable capitulation to a garrison which has resisted stoutly than to assault.

XLVII.

Infantry, cavalry and artillery, can never do without each other; they should, therefore, be so cantoned as always to aid one another in case of surprise.

XLVIII.

The infantry ought to be formed in two lines only, for the musket cannot be used with effect except under this disposition, and it is recognised that the fire of the third line is very imperfect and even injurious to that of the two in front. In forming the infantry into two lines you must allow one of serrefiles of a ninth of the whole effective, *i.e.*, one every yard; a reserve to be placed twelve yards behind the flanks.

XLIX.

The method of mixing platoons of infantry with cavalry is wrong altogether; it will only result in mischief. The cavalry ceases to be mobile; it is trammelled in all its movements, it loses its impulse. The infantry, too, is affected, for at the first movement of the cavalry, it is unsupported. The best method of protecting cavalry is by protecting its flanks.

L.

Cavalry charges are equally good at the commencement, the middle, and the end of the battle; they should be made as often as possible on the flanks of the infantry, especially when the latter is engaged in front.*

LI.

It is for the cavalry to follow up the beaten enemy and prevent his rallying.

LII.

Artillery is more necessary for cavalry than for infantry, since cavalry cannot return fire, nor fight except with sabre. It is to supply this deficiency that horse artillery have been created. Cavalry should always have its batteries with it, whether attacking, remaining in position, or rallying.

LIII.

In march or position the greatest part of the artillery ought to be with the infantry and cavalry divisions; the remainder should be held in reserve. Each gun should have 300 rounds, not counting the waggon reserve; this supply will do for two battles.

LIV.

Batteries should be placed in the most advantageous positions, and as far as possible in front of the lines of infantry and cavalry, without these latter being at all endangered. The batteries should command the country from the height of the platform—they should not be shut off (masked) on the right or left—so that they can open fire in any direction.

---

* Very great attention is being again given to the successful co-operation of cavalry in battle, and its great value in action, after the infantry employed has expended the whole of its small ammunition, in these our days of quick firing. The great difficulty in leading cavalry now-a-days is to move it over considerable distances, so as to bring it into collision with the enemy at the right moment. It is a wise step that all cavalry be armed with the lance, instead of only one squadron in each regiment, at any rate all light horse should be taught the lance exercise. (L. E. H.)

LV.

A general should avoid placing his army in billets when he has the means of getting together magazines of stores and forage, and so satisfying the wants of his soldiers.

LVI.

A good general, with a good staff, organization, instruction, and with severe discipline, can make good troops—independently of the cause for which they are fighting. Yet enthusiasm, love of the fatherland national pride, will stir young troops.

LVII.

When a nation has no staff of officers, and no principle of military organization, it will be difficult for it to form an army.

LVIII.

The first quality of a soldier is fortitude in enduring fatigue and hardship; bravery—but the second. Poverty, hardship and misery, are the school of the good soldier.

LIX.

There are five things which the soldier must never let from him:—his gun, ammunition, knapsack, provisions for at least four days, and pioneering tools. Let him, if he thinks fit, have his knapsack of the least possible size, but have it with him always.

LX.

Soldiers must be encouraged in all ways to remain with the colours; this you will attain by showing great esteem for soldiers. The pay should also be increased in proportion to the years of service, for it is a great injustice not to pay a veteran more than a recruit.

LXI.

Orations, when at the point of fighting, do not make a soldier brave; old soldiers hardly listen, and recruits forget themselves at the first cannon shot. If addresses and reasoning are of any service, it is during the course of a campaign, in order to prevent rumours and false reports, to maintain a good spirit in the camp, and to furnish materials for conversation at the bivouacs. The printed order of the day should fulfil these different objects.

LXII.

Tents are not healthy. It is better for the soldier to camp out, for he sleeps with feet to the fire, the proximity of which soon dries the ground on which he lies, some planks and a little straw protect him from the wind. However, the tent is necessary for the commanders, who need to write and consult the maps; they should, therefore, be given to superiors, who should be ordered never to sleep in a house. Tents are objects of observation to the enemy's staff, and they give him information as to your number and position. But an army with two or three lines of bivouacs show nothing at a distance but smoke, which the enemy would confound with the mists of the atmosphere; it is impossible to count the number of fires.

LXIII.

Information obtained from prisoners should be priced at the right value; a soldier sees nothing beyond his company, and the officer at most can give an account of the movements and position of the division to which his regiment belongs. Thus a general in command should not consider confessions torn from prisoners, except when they square with the reports of the outposts, to justify his conjectures as to the position the enemy occupies.

LXIV.

Nothing is more important in war than unity in the command; thus when there is war against but one power there should be but one army, acting on one line, and led by one chief.

LXV.

After too much talk, uncertainty, difficulty and consultation, what has happened in all centuries, when pursuing a like line, will again take place; *i.e.*, that one ends in taking the worst course, which almost always in war is the most pusillanimous—or, if you will, the most prudent. True wisdom for a general lies in energy and resolution.

LXVI.

In war, the leader alone understands the importance of certain things, and he may alone, of his own will and superior wisdom, conquer and overcome all difficulties.

LXVII.

Allowing generals and officers to lay down arms, as the result of a particular capitulation, except when they form the garrison of a fortified place, leads the way to undeniable difficulties. It is destructive to the military spirit of a nation thus to open a way to cowardly or timid men, or even to brave men who have strayed. In an extraordinary position, extraordinary resolution is needed; the more important the resistance of any body, the better are its chances of being succoured or of cutting its way through. How many things which appeared impossible, have been done by resolute men, whose only other resource was to die!

LXVIII.

No Sovereign or people can have security if it permits officers to capitulate on the field, and to lay down their arms on conditions favourable to the concerned, but opposed to the interests of the remainder of the army. To get out of danger oneself, to make that of one's companions more perilous, is clearly cowardice; such action should be proscribed, made infamous, and be visited with the death-penalty. Generals, officers and soldiers, who in battle have saved their lives by capitulation, should be shot down; both he who orders a surrender, and those who obey the order, are traitors alike, and deserve capital punishment.*

LXIX.

There is but one honourable way of being made a prisoner of war, it is when one is taken by oneself, and when unable any longer to use one's arms. Then there are no conditions, because to make them with honour is impossible, but one is compelled to surrender by absolute necessity.

LXX.

The course of a general in a conquered country is like a ship surrounded by rocks. If he is harsh he irritates and increases the number of his enemies; if he is too mild, he causes the abuses and vexations inevitably attached to the art of war, to show themselves in a more acute form. A conqueror should know how to employ in turn severity, justice and leniency, both to calm and prevent seditions.

LXXI.

Nothing can excuse a general taking advantage of knowledge gained in the service of his country, to fight against it, and to deliver its ramparts to foreign nations; this crime is condemned by the principles of religion, morality, and honour.

---

* *See* Foot-Notes, pp. **100, 119, 134, 160.** (L. E. H.)

LXXII.

A commander-in-chief is not protected for his faults in war, by the order of his Sovereign or of a Minister, when it is given by one distant from the field of operations, or ill, perhaps not at all, acquainted with the last turn matters have taken. Whence it follows that every such commander who undertakes to carry out a plan he thinks bad, is guilty; he should represent his motives, insist on the plan being changed, in fine, resign rather than be the instrument of the ruin of his army. Every commander-in-chief who, in consequence of orders from above, fights feeling certain that he will lose, is equally guilty. In this last case he should refuse to obey, because an order in war only demands implicit obedience when given by a superior who, the moment he gives it, is present at the seat of war, being then acquainted with the state of things; he may listen to objections and give all necessary explanations to the officer who is to carry the order out. But if a commander receives a distinct order from his Sovereign to deliver battle, with an injunction to yield the victory to his opponent, ought he to obey? No. If the general understands the reason for this strange order he should execute it, but if not he should refuse to obey.

LXXIII.

The first quality of a commander is a cool head, which will judge things in a true light; he should not let himself be dazed by good or bad news; the sensations he receives successively, or once during the course of a day, should be classed in the memory so as to occupy only the place they deserve, for reasoning and judgment are but the result of many sensations equally considered. There are men who from their nature, physical or moral, make of each thing a complete picture, whatever may be their skill or talent or courage ; nature has not called them to the command of armies and to the direction of the great operations of war.

LXXIV.

To know the map perfectly, to understand reconnoitring, to take care that orders are carried out, to present in a simple manner the most complex movements of an army—these are the qualities befitting an officer called to serve on the Staff of the General in command.

LXXV.

It is the duty of the general of artillery to know of all the operations of the army, since he has to furnish arms and ammunition to the different divisions composing it. His intercourse with the commanders of artillery at the outposts should keep him acquainted with all the movements of the army ; and the action of his main artillery park should depend on the information thus gained.

LXXVI.

To have a quick eye for defiles and fords, to secure good guides, to examine the priest and the postmaster, to have quick communication with the inhabitants, to dispatch scouts, to seize letters, translate and analyze them ; finally, to answer all the great questions of the commander-in-chief; such are the qualities befitting a good general commanding the outposts.

LXXVII.

Generals-in-chief are guided by their own experience or genius. Tactics, evolutions, the science of an artillery or engineering officer may be picked up from books,*

---

* Witness the large number of military teachers whose reports set all their brother officers' imagination in a blaze ; and yet these teachers—even not once as *per amusare la bocca*—have never " sniffed " the lickerish savour of gunpowder " under fire." (L. E. H.)

but the knowledge of the great operations of war can only be acquired by experience, and by the applied study of the campaigns of all the great captains. Gustavus, Turenne and Frederick, as well as Alexander, Hannibal and Cæsar, have all acted on the same principles. To keep one's forces together, to bear speedily on any point, to be nowhere vulnerable, such are the principles that assure victory; to inspire fear by the reputation of one's arms, that is what maintains the fidelity of allies, and the obedience of conquered nations.

LXXVIII.

Read and re-read the Campaigns of Alexander, Hannibal, Cæsar, Gustavus Adolphus, Turenne, Eugène and Frederick; take them for your model, that is the only way of becoming a great captain, to obtain the secrets of the art of war.

BOOK II.

LXXIX.

The first principle of a commander-in-chief is to observe clearly what he does, to see if he has all the means of surmounting any obstacle the enemy may place in his way, and if he has made up his mind to do all to overcome those obstacles.

LXXX.

The art of a general, commanding in the van or in the rear, is, without imperilling himself, to keep the enemy back, to delay him, to make him employ three or four hours in marching a league. Tactics alone can give the means of attaining these ends; it is more necessary to cavalry than to infantry, in the van or rear, than in any other position.

LXXXI.

It is rare, and difficult, to possess at one time all the qualities of a great general. What is most desirable (because that draws a man out at once of the common line) is to maintain an equilibrium between his mind and abilities, and his will and courage. If courage prevails more in his composition, the general will undertake designs, the whole possibility of the attainment of which he has not thought out; on the other hand he will not dare to carry his ideas into execution, if his will or courage is inferior to his abilities.

LXXXII.

With a great general, no great action is executed, which is the fruit of chance, or fortune; they are all the result of combination and talent.

LXXXIII.

A commander-in-chief never gives rest either to the victor or to the conquered.

LXXXIV.

An irresolute general who acts without principles or plan, although at the head of an army superior in number to that of the foe, often proves inferior in the battle field. Shuffling, half-measures, lose everything in war.

LXXXV.

To a talented general who has to think out, propose, and execute everything by himself, good judgment and a solid mind are necessary.

LXXXVI.

A cavalry general should possess practical knowledge, know the preciousness of a second even of time, despise life and not trust to chance.

LXXXVII.

A general in the hands of the foe has no power to give orders; to obey them is criminal.

LXXXVIII.

Cavalry of the line should be posted in van, rear, wings, and reserve to support the light cavalry.

LXXXIX.

To wish to keep cavalry for the end of the fight, betrays no idea of the effective power of the charges combined of cavalry and infantry either for attack or defence.

XC.

The strength of cavalry lies in its impetus; but speed alone does not insure victory: what does, is order, harmony, and the proper employment of the reserves.

XCI.

The cavalry should bear a proportion to the infantry of one-fourth in Flanders or Germany; one-twentieth on the Pyrenees or Alps; one-sixth in Italy or Spain.

XCII.

In battle, as in a siege, art is shown in directing fire from many quarters on one point; when the fight is once begun, a leader skilful enough to bring to bear on one such point, unknown to the foe, an unexpected mass of artillery, is sure to carry the day.

XCIII.

The better the infantry, the greater the need to husband it, and support it by good batteries. Good infantry is without doubt the backbone of an army, but if it has had to fight for some length of time against very superior artillery, it will be demoralized and destroyed. It may be that a general, a more skilful manœuvrer than his opponent, may, with his superior infantry, be successful in a part of the campaign, although his artillery is much inferior; but, at the crisis of a general engagement he will bitterly feel his weakness in artillery.

XCIV.

A good army of 35,000 to 40,000 men, should in a few days, especially when flanked by a great town or river, render its position unattackable by an army twice its number.

XCV.

War is made up of accidents, and although bound to follow general principles, a general ought not to lose from sight anything which may enable him to profit from these accidents; it is a characteristic of talent. In war there is but one favourable moment: the great thing is to seize it.

XCVI.

A general who keeps fresh troops for the day after the battle almost always is beaten; one must employ, if useful, one's very last man, because, on the day after a complete success, there is no obstacle left; public opinion alone is enough indeed to secure fresh triumphs to the victor.

XCVII.

The rules of war demand that a division of an army should avoid fighting alone a whole army which has already scored success.

XCVIII.

When a general has forestalled the investment of a place, has gained a few days on his opponent, he should profit thereby to surround himself by lines of circumvallation; from that moment he has bettered his position, and has acquired, in the general condition of affairs, a new degree of strength, a new element of force.

XCIX.

In war a commandant of a place is not a judge of events; he should hold till the last moment; he deserves death when he surrenders an instant sooner than he is obliged.

C.

Capitulations of bodies, who are cut off during a battle, or on active campaign, are contracts, of which the advantage comes to the contracting parties, but the onerous conditions fall on the prince and the other soldiers. To get out of danger oneself, to make the general's position more dangerous, is clear cowardice.

CI.

Defensive war does not exclude attack, just as offensive war does not exclude defence, although its aim is to force the frontier and invade the enemy's country.

CII.

The art of war points out that it is necessary to turn and outflank a wing without separating the army.

CIII.

Field fortifications are always of use, never hurtful, when they are well understood.

CIV.

An army can pass always and in every season wherever there is room for two men's feet.

CV.

The conditions of the position occupied should not alone decide the order of battle, which should be determined by the whole circumstances.

CVI.

Flank marches are to be avoided, and when made should be as short and in as brief a time as possible.

CVII.

Nothing is more calculated to disorganise and ruin an army altogether than plundering.

CVIII.

An enemy's praise is suspicious; it is only flattery to a man of honour when given after the cessation of war.

CIX.

Prisoners of war belong no more to the power for which they have fought; they are all under the safeguard and protection of the honour and generosity of the nation which has disarmed them.

CX.

Conquered provinces should be kept in obedience to their conquerors by moral means, such as making the parishes responsible and establishing a sound administration. Hostages are one of the most powerful of these means, but then they should be numerous and chosen from the chief men; and inhabitants should understand that the death of the hostages would be the immediate consequence of the violation of faith.

CXI.

The physical configuration of the country; whether living on the mountains or in the plains; the education or discipline of the inhabitants, have more effect than climate on the character of the troops.

CXII.

All the great captains have done their great deeds by conforming to the rules and natural principles of their art, and by the soundness of their plans, and the proportioned connection maintained between their means and the results they expect, between their efforts and the obstacles to be overcome. They have only succeeded by conforming to rules, whatever might have been the boldness of their designs and the extent of their success. It is on this ground alone that they are our models, and it is only by imitating them that we can hope to rival them.

CXIII.

The first law of maritime tactics should be that, as soon as the admiral has given the signal, each captain should be prepared to make the necessary evolutions for attack of an enemy's ship, to take part in the fight, and support his neighbours.

CXIV.

War on land destroys, in general, more men than war at sea; it is more perilous. The sailor in a squadron fights but once in a campaign; the soldier fights always. The sailor, whatever may be the dangers and hardships of his element, has less to endure than the soldier. He has with him always his abode, kitchen, hospital, dispensary. The naval armies in the services of France and England, where discipline maintains cleanliness, and to whom experience has taught all the necessary measures for the preservation of health, have fewer men on the sick list than land armies. Independently of danger of fighting, the sailor has that of the sea; but art has so much diminished this latter that it cannot be compared to the perils of the land, popular risings, individual murder, being cut off, surprises by the enemy's light troops, &c.

CXV.

A general, commanding-in-chief a naval army, and a chief of a land army are men who need different qualities. The qualities for the latter are inborn, but those for the former are acquired by experience alone. The art of land warfare is an art of genius, and inspirations. In maritime war nothing depends on genius and inspiration, all is positive, a matter of experience. The sea-general has but need of one science—navigation. The land-commander has need of all, or of equivalent to all, *e.g.*, that of profiting by universal experience and knowledge. The one has nothing to guess, he knows the position and strength of his antagonists. The other knows nothing for certain, never sees his foe, does not know exactly where he is. When the armies are face to face, the least accident of the ground, the smallest wood, will hide a part of the army. The most practised eye cannot tell if he sees the whole of the hostile army, or but three-quarters. It is by the eyes of the mind, the conjoint use of his reasoning powers, that he sees, knows, and judges. The naval commander has no need of a practised eye, none of the enemy's forces are hidden from him. That which makes the work of the land-commander so difficult is the necessity of feeding so many men and animals; if he will not submit to being guided by the commissaries, he will not be able to stir an inch, and his designs will fail. He of the sea is never so embarrassed; he carries everything with him. He has not to reconnoitre, no ground to examine, no battle-field to study. The Indian Ocean, and the American Ocean, the Channel, all are but same liquid. The most skilled have no advantage over the least, except by the knowledge of the winds prevailing in such and such a quarter, by foreseeing those which ought to prevail, or by atmospheric signs; qualifications acquired by experience, and by experience alone. The land commandant never knows the battle field where he is to operate. His glance is an experienced one, he has no positive information, the data given to him to arrive at a knowledge of localities are so casual that almost nothing is taught by experience. It is the faculty of seizing at once the connection which the ground bears to the nature of countries, it is a gift termed "*the soldier's eye*," which great generals have received from Nature; yet the observations made on topographical charts, the ease given by education and habit of reading from them, may be of some assistance.

A naval commander depends more on his captains than a land commander on his generals. This latter is in a position to take on himself the direct command of the troops to bear on all points, and of remedying false moves. A naval general, personally, has influence but over the men of his own ship. The smoke prevents the signals from being seen, the winds change or are not the same over all space covered by his line. It is then, of all professions, the one in which subalterns may take the most on themselves.*

---

* Napoléon knew little about Naval Affairs. Sailors may exclaim *Mirabile dictu !* about those Naval Counsels of his. (L. E. H.)

PART II.

ILLUSTRATION OF THE MAXIMS.

BOOK I.

I.

Napoléon, in his military career, seems to have been called upon to surmount all the difficulties of a war of invasion. In Egypt, he crossed the desert, conquered and destroyed the Mamelukes, so much to be praised for their skill and valour; he bent his genius to all the dangers of this far-off expedition, in a country where everything was opposed to the wants of his army. To conquer Italy he twice crossed the Alps, in the most difficult passes and at a season which multiplied those difficulties. In three months he passed the Pyrenees, beat and dispersed four Spanish Armies. Lastly, from the banks of the Rhine to those of the Borysthenes, no natural barrier has been found able to bar the rapid march of his victorious legions.

II.

Sometimes success attends a plan of campaign which is hazardous and contrary to the principles of the art of war; but such success usually depends on the caprices of fortune, or on the mistakes of the enemy, two things on which we cannot always count.

Although based on the true principles of war, a plan of campaign decided beforehand runs a chance of failure, if the opponent, who, after being on the defensive, takes the initiative, and improvises skilful manœuvres. Such was the plan sketched by the Aulic Council for the campaign of 1796, conducted by Marshal Wurmser. The great numerical superiority of his army made him hope for the complete destruction of the French army, whose retreat also he wished to cut off; Wurmser based his operations on the defensive situation of his antagonist, who, posted on the line of the Adige, had to cover the siege of Mantua, and middle and lower Italy. Wurmser, supposing the French Army fixed round Mantua, formed his army into three corps, who were separately to form a junction there. Napoléon having guessed the designs of the Austrian general, felt the whole advantage given him by taking the initiative over an army divided into three bodies, and with no communications. He hastened to raise the siege of Mantua, collected his whole strength, and thereby found himself superior to the Imperial army, whose divisions he attacked in detail and defeated. Thus Wurmser, who at first had dreamt only of a victory he deemed certain, was compelled, after 10 days' campaign, to retire the wreck of his army into the Tyrol, after losing 25,000 men killed or wounded, 15,000 prisoners, 66 pieces of cannon and nine standards.

Nothing is then more difficult than to trace out in advance for a commander the action he is to pursue during a campaign; for, besides that success often depends on unforeseen circumstances, the inspirations of genius are stifled by making the chief of an army act on another's direction.

III.

These general principles of the art were totally forgotten or unknown in the wars of the middle ages. The Crusaders, in their numerous invasions of Palestine, seemed to have had no other aim but to fight and conquer, so little pains did they take to profit from victory; thus numberless armies went and perished in Syria, without getting any results therefrom but the more or less transitory successes, gained usually by their superior number.

It was also by forgetting these principles that Charles XII., abandoning his line of operation and communication with Sweden, threw himself into the Ukraine, where he lost the greater part of his army by the hardships of a winter campaign in a country, desert and destitute of resources. Beaten at Pultava, he had to seek refuge in Turkey by crossing the Dnieper, with the wreck of his army, amounting to a little more than 1,000 men.

Gustavus was the first to bring such war to its true principles. His operations in Germany were boldly, swiftly, and well ordered; he was skilled in employing victory to shelter himself from defeat, and his line of operation was so arranged as to guard against anything that might happen, and to maintain his communication with Sweden. His campaigns are a new era in the history of war.

IV.

In the campaign of 1757, marching to the conquest of Bohemia with two armies, each with its own line of operation, he succeeded in forming a junction in sight of the Duke of Lorraine, who was covering Prague with the Imperial army, but this example is not one to follow. The success of this march depended entirely on the Duke, who, with 70,000 men, made no effort to prevent the junction of the two Prussian armies.

V.

Marshal de Villars has said that when there is a risk of war exact information should be obtained of the troops possessed by the Sovereign against whom one has to fight, because it is not possible to form sound designs, either for the offensive or defensive, without precise knowledge as to what one might hope or fear. When the first cannon-shots are fired one cannot know what will be the end of the war; thus we must think well before commencing it. Yet once we have decided on it Villars observes "that the greatest and boldest plans are often the wisest and luckiest. When one would make war," he adds, "one must make it well; and above all, no shuffling!"

VI.

The opinion of Marshal Saxe is that there can be no great retreat except when the enemy follows slowly; for if he pursues hotly, the retreat will be turned into a rout. "It is then a great thing," says the Marshal, "for us to adopt the proverb—'we must make a bridge of gold for our enemy'—since we are sure to destroy him if a vigorous charge is made as soon as he begins to retreat."*

VII.

The following maxims, taken from the memoirs of Montecuculli, seem to me to have their place here to serve as a supplement to the general principles given in this paragraph.

1st.—Once war is decided on, we should attend no longer to doubts or scruples, and think that all the evil which might happen does not always happen, either because Providence may divert it, our wisdom avoid it, or our enemy's foresight not perceive it. It assures the success of a campaign to give the command-in-chief to one man, because, when authority is divided, there are so many different opinions and want of connection in the

---

* It might be supposed by some that the Marshal did not understand the proverb then. If there was *no* line of retreat, the enemy cannot retreat and thus *may* fight it out and *win*. (L. E. H.)

operations. Besides, the enterprise being considered a common one and not peculiar to ourselves, we do not execute it with so much energy.

After having followed all the rules of the art, and feeling convinced that nothing has been forgotten to secure the success of our designs, we must leave the issue to Providence and hide our soul in peace for what it may please God to ordain.*

(1.) A general-in-chief, whatever may happen, should remain firm and resolute in his designs; he should avoid alike arrogance in victory and dejection in adversity; for, in war, success and defeat follow closely on one another, and make a continual ebb and flow.

(2.) When an army is brave and hardened, and that of the enemy is weak and raw, or rather demoralized by long idleness, we should try to force a battle. If, however, the enemy has the advantage in troops, a decisive fight is to be avoided, and we should camp in a favourable position, entrench in defiles, and be content in barring his advance. When the armies are almost equal, a fight should not be avoided, but sought to be engaged advantageously; for this we must camp in front of the enemy, keep level with him in marching by heights and advantageous places, seize castles and passes round the camp, and post oneself advantageously in the places where we are to pass; it is very good if we can prevent him from doing anything, make him lose time, destroy his designs, or delay their progress and execution. Lastly, if an army is altogether inferior to that of the foe, and there is no possibility of manœuvring against it with advantage, the campaign should be abandoned and a retreat made into strong posts.

---

* Empty talk.—An honest man should add "Throw your whole heart and soul and energy into the work." (L. E. H.)

(3.) The principal care of a general commanding at a battle, should be to secure his flanks. Natural positions may indeed effect this ; but, being immovable, they can only be of use to one awaiting the enemy's onslaught, but not to one who marches to meet him. It is then by the arrangement of his troops that a general is to put himself into a position to repel attacks on his front, flank, or rear.

If one of the flanks is supported by a river or inaccessable ravine, all the cavalry may be posted on the other, so that by superiority in numbers, the enemy might more easily be surrounded. If the enemy has one of his flanks protected by woods, light cavalry or infantry should be dispatched in the thick of the battle to attack him in flank or rear, and, if feasible, the baggage may be stormed and thrown into confusion.

If it is desired to beat the enemy's right with one's left, or his left with one's right, the attacking wing should be reinforced and with picked troops ; on marching against the foe, the general should refuse to engage the wing, which is not to fight, while he will push the other on swiftly in order to crush his antagonist. When the nature of the ground permits, he should approach stealthily and attack before the enemy is on the defence.

If signs of fear are perceptible in the enemy, which may be known by his disorder and confusion, immediate pursuit is necessary, so that he cannot recover ; then, too, the cavalry should be so manœuvred as to cut off the enemy's artillery and baggage.

(4.) The order of march should be subordinated to the order of battle sketched beforehand. The march is well ordered when it is proportioned to the road that has to be traversed, and to the time one has to traverse it.

The front is extended or contracted according to the topography of the place, care being taken to keep the artillery on the high roads.

When a river is to be crossed, the artillery in batteries should be posted on the bank, opposite to the point where it is intended to cross; it would be a great advantage if the river made a bend there, and if there is a ford at the place where the passage is to be effected. As the bridge is built, the infantry is sent on to fire on the other side to protect the workers; as soon as it is completed, some infantry, cavalry, and cannon are to be dispatched. The infantry should immediately entrench at the end of the bridge, and it is even prudent to fortify on this side of the stream, to protect the bridge in case the enemy attempted the offensive.

The vanguards should have good guides and pioneers, the one to point the easy passes and the other to make them practicable. If the army marches by detachments, each of the commanders should have written notice as to the place of junction of the army, which should be far enough from the foe to prevent him seizing it before junction is made. Therefore, it should be kept secret.

An army should march in the same order as it is to fight in as soon as the enemy is approached. If there is anything to be feared, care should be proportioned to the magnitude of the fear. When a defile is passed, the troops should halt till all have passed.

To hide one's movements, march should be by night, through woods and valleys. Covered ground is to be sought, inhabited places avoided; no fires; order of departure to be given verbally—such are the precautions in these cases. When the object is to carry a post or to throw oneself into a besieged place, the van should march at gun shot distance, for then one should be prepared to crush all obstacles one may meet.

When the march is to force a passage guarded by the enemy, a feint should be made of driving him in one direction and, by a quiet manœuvre, dash into another. Success is often gained by appearing to retrace one's steps, and then by a sudden counter-march seizing the passage before the enemy has occupied it. Some generals have forced passages by manœuvring before the enemy, while a detachment surprised the passage, stealing a march by the aid of the nature of the ground, the enemy, occupied in observing your passage, allows the detachment to entrench in the post he has found necessary to occupy.

(5.) An army camps differently, according to the dangers to be dreaded, and the precautions thereby needed. When it is in friendly country it camps separately, to give greater convenience to the soldiers, but if the enemy is at hand, it should camp in order of battle. It is necessary as much as possible to cover one side of the camp by some natural protection, such as a river, a group of rocks, or a ravine; care must be taken to prevent the camp from being commanded, and any bar being put to the intercommunication of the different quarters, so that the troops should be always in a position to help one another.

When an army stays in camp there should be a supply of provisions and ammunition, and a supply should be easily brought there; to do so it must well establish its lines of communication and take care not to leave behind it a hostile post.

When an army has gone into winter quarters the safety of the troops is assured, either by choosing a camp and fortifying it; and for this one must be near to a great trading town, or a river, to facilitate transports; or by posting the troops in narrow places so that the cantonments are close to one another, whereby the soldiers can support one another. Winter quarters are also covered by constructing small closed out-works along the avenues of cantonments and placing there cavalry outposts to observe the enemy's movements.

(6.) One seeks for battle when there is reason to hope for victory, or a fear of ruin to one's army by not fighting to relieve a besieged place; to prevent assistance coming to the foe. Battles are useful when one wishes to profit by an advantage which presents itself, *e.g.*, to seize an opportunity to overwhelm the enemy when he has just committed a fault, or when division among the leaders makes the movements favourable for attack.

If the enemy declines battle, it may be forced by besieging an important place, or by making a sudden charge when he cannot easily effect his retreat; or by feigning to retire, then, by a quick counter-measure, suddenly attacking him and compelling him to fight. The different cases to refuse or avoid battle are when more is to be lost by defeat than to be gained by triumph; when there is too great an inferiority to the foe and help is awaited; lastly, when the enemy is well posted, or when the chances are that he will destroy himself either by a faulty position or thanks to the misunderstandings between the chiefs.

To gain a battle each arm should be advantageously posted, and one should be in a condition to fight, in front or flank, without supporting the wings by natural obstacles, if they be at hand, or even if there be need by works of art. One must take care that the troops should support one another without confusion, and that those that are broken are not forced back on the others. Intervals should be maintained between the different bodies, but not big enough to allow the enemy to penetrate, because then the reserves would have to be brought up, and there would be danger of a rout. Victory is sometimes obtained by making a diversion in the middle of a battle, or, again, by depriving the soldier of all hope of retreat, and putting him into a position where he has nothing to do but to conquer or die.

At the beginning of a battle you should go for the enemy if the ground is level, in order to give confidence to the soldiers, but if well posted, and the artillery is advantageously placed, you may await him firmly. Lastly, you must fight with determination, help, when wanted, the fatigued, and only bring up the reserves at the last extremity, leaving always some support on which broken troops may rally.

When obliged to attack with all one's forces, the engagement should take place in the evening, for then, whatever be the issue of the battle, night will come and separate the combatants before the troops are too tired; thereby power is obtained to effect a retreat if the issue of the fight so obliges.*

During a battle the general-in-chief should occupy a position from which he can see, as far as possible, his whole army; he should be informed on the spot of all that happens in the different divisions. His duty is to distribute assistance, to make success decisive at points where the enemy wavers, and to reinforce his troops where they are giving way. When the enemy is beaten he should be pursued before he has time to rally; on the other hand, when all hope of victory has been abandoned, a retreat should be made with as much order as possible.

(7.) It shows great talent in a general to engage his prepared troops with unprepared ones, his fresh men with a fatigued enemy, his brave and disciplined soldiers

---
* Although losing the value of the victory if successful. (L. E. H.)

with their recruits. He should be swift to fall with his army on a weak and detached body, to follow the enemy's trail, to charge him in the defiles before he can turn round and form a line of battle.

(8.) A position is advantageous, when all the arms are so placed that they can do their work, with none remaining idle. A position should be taken in plains and uncovered grounds, if the army has great strength in cavalry; if it is stronger in infantry, in places covered and difficult; in narrow places if it has inferiority in troops, and in wide expanses if it is superior in numbers. With an army altogether inferior a difficult post should be found, occupied, and entrenched. To gain all the possible advantage out of a diversion, it is to be observed that the country, upon which it is to be made, should be easily invaded. It should be carried out with energy, and in places where it can inflict the greatest damage on the foe.

(9.) To wage war well, it is not necessary then to abandon the following general principles : to be stronger than the enemy in numbers and *moral;* to give battle only to strike terror into the country; to divide the army into as many bodies as may be made without risk, in order to undertake several things at one time ; to treat well those that surrender, but sternly those that hold out ; to secure one's rear, to establish and strengthen oneself in some post, which will serve as a general rallying centre wherefrom to operate in all future movements. Large rivers, passages of all kinds should be got hold of, and the line of communications established through securing both fortified places by a siege and the open country by battle. It is indeed useless to try to gain great victories without the trouble of big fighting.

But a general should at times know how to make use both of compulsory and gentle means in order to keep safe the fruit of his victories and conquests.

VIII.

In the campaign of 1758 the position of the Prussian army at Hohenkirch, commanded by hostile batteries which occupied all the heights, was an eminently faulty one. Yet Frederick, who saw his rear menaced by Laudon's Corps, remained six days in the camp without seeking to rectify his position. It does not appear that he perceived all his danger, for Marshal Daun, having manœuvred all night so as to attack at dawn, surprised the Prussians in their camp before they could put themselves on their defence; they were surrounded on all sides. Frederick succeeded indeed in effecting his retreat, but with a loss of 10,000 men, many generals, and almost all his artillery. If the Marshal had followed up his success more boldly the king would never have been able to rally; his good fortune saved him from dangers, to which his want of foresight had exposed him.

Marshal Saxe has said, however, that there is more skill than one thinks in making bad dispositions, if they can be changed into good at the right moment. Nothing astonishes the enemy more than this manœuvre; he has counted on a certain thing, he has arranged accordingly, and now when about to attack, he knows nothing for certain. "I repeat it," says the Marshal, "nothing disconcerts an enemy more, and makes him commit faults; for it follows that if he does not alter his dispositions he is beaten, and if he does change them in presence of his antagonist, he is no less defeated."

It seems to me that a general who would rest the success of a battle on such principles would run more chance of losing than winning, for if he has to deal with a skilled and artful adversary, the latter might find time enough to profit by his bad dispositions before they could be rectified.

IX.

Swiftness, says Montecuculli, is of use to keep secret the operations of an army, because it leaves no time to divulge the intentions of the chief. It is advantageous to burst on the unguarded enemy, surprise him, and strike him with the thunderbolt before he has seen the lightning. But if too great speed weakens, and delay takes away the favourable occasion, you must weigh the good and evil, one each side, and choose.

Marshal de Villars used to say that in war all depends upon imposing on the enemy, and when this point is gained, giving him no time to recover heart. Villars has conjoined example with precept, for his bold and swift operations were always attended with success. The advice of Frederick was that wars should be short and sharp, because a long war weakens discipline, gradually unpeoples the state, and wastes resources.

X.

The campaign of 1814 in France was ably designed on these principles. Napoléon, with an army inferior in number and discouraged by the disastrous retreats from Moscow and Leipzig, and more so by the presence of the enemy on French ground, yet succeeded in making good his immense inferiority by swift and well-combined manœuvres. The successes gained at Champaubert, Montmirail, Montereau, Rheims, began to raise the *morale* of the French army: the numerous recruits of which it was formed were already gaining the steadiness of veteran regiments, when the capture of Paris and the astonishing revolution it brought about forced Napoléon to lay down arms. This result depended rather on the pressure of circumstances than on absolute necessity; Napoléon indeed, by betaking himself to the other side of the Loire, might have easily effected his junction with the armies off the Alps and the Pyrenees, and re-appeared on the field of battle with 100,000 combatants. This force was quite enough to restore the chances in his favour, and more so because the armies of the allied Sovereigns were manœuvring on the French frontier with their backs to all the fortresses of France and Italy.*

XI.

The Austrian army, under the orders of Field Marshal Alvinzi, divided into two bodies, acting independently, to join before Mantua. The first, 85,000 strong, was under the orders of Alvinzi; he was to emerge by Montebaldo near the position of the French army on the Adige. The second, under General Provera, was to act on the base of the Adige and relieve Mantua. Napoléon, informed as to the enemy's movements but not yet understanding his designs, confined himself to concentrating his troops and ordering them to be ready to manœuvre. However, fresh information soon showed the commander-in-chief of the French army that the division which had emerged by the Corona on Montebaldo sought to form a junction with its cavalry and artillery, which, after crossing the Adige and Dolo, was marching on to the plateau of Rivoli by the causeway, at Incanole. Napoléon judged that once master of this plateau, he could oppose their junction and turn in his favour all the chances of the initiative; he set the troops on the march, and at 2 a.m. had occupied this important position. Having got possession of the point of junction

---

* Why did he not do it ? *Qui trop embrasse mal étreint*, is the reply. (L. E. 11.)

of the Austrian columns, success followed his dispositions; he repulsed all their attacks, made 7,000 prisoners, took twelve pieces of cannon and several standards.

It was 2 a.m., the battle of Rivoli was gained, when Napoléon learnt that General Provera had crossed the Adige at Anghiari and was marching on Mantua. He gave up to his lieutenants the task of following up the pursuit of Alvinzi, and put himself at the head of a division to frustrate the designs of Provera. By a quick march he succeeded in gaining the initiative once more, and in preventing the garrison of Mantua from joining the army of relief; moreover, the body entrusted with the blockade, proud of fighting under the eyes of the victor of Rivoli, forced the garrison to retire into the place. At the same time Victor's division, forgetting the fatigues of a forest march, impetuously attacked the front of the army of relief, while a sortie from the lines of St. George pressed hard on the flank, and the division of Augereau, which had followed the march of the Austrian general, attacked him on the rear. Provera, surrounded on all sides, capitulated. The result of these two battles cost Austria 3,000 men, killed or wounded, 22,000 prisoners, 46 pieces of cannon, and 24 standards.

XII.

"An army's line of communication should be sure and well settled," says Montecuculli; for every army which departs from its line and takes no care of this connecting passage, open and assured, marches on the edge of a precipice; it is seeking ruin as appears by numberless examples. Indeed, if the road by which provisions and supplies of men and ammunition arrive is not assured, if the magazines, hospitals, arsenals and market places are not fixed and situated conveniently, not only will the

XIII.

When an army marches at a distance from the enemy, its columns may proceed by the high roads, in order to husband the artillery and vehicles; but if it marches to fight, the different corps must be formed in serried line of battle. The general should, moreover, see that the heads of columns intended to attack together do not get in advance of one another, and that, on approach to the battle-field, they maintain between each a distance sufficient to allow them to deploy. "Fighting demands much caution," said Frederick; thus he recommended his generals to keep on their guard and to examine the ground at a distance, to take the initiative and seize positions which may favour an attack.

In a retreat many generals advise a concentration of strength and a march in serried column if there is still strength enough to re-seize the offensive; for thereby it is easy to form for a battle when a position is favourable, either to stay the enemy when aid is expected, or to attack him if he is not equal to the fight. Such was the retreat of Moreau after the passage of the Adda by the Austro-Russian army. The French general, after having covered the evacuation of Milan, took up a position between the Po and the Tanaro; his camp, which was flanked by Alessandria and Valencia—two excellent military posts—had the advantage of covering the roads to Turin and Savona, by which he wished to effect his retreat in case he should not succeed in making his junction with the divisions of Macdonald, who had received orders to quit the kingdom of Naples and to hasten his return into Tuscany. Forced to leave this position by reason of the rising of Piedmont and

Tuscany, Moreau retired on Asti, where he learnt that his communication with the Gulf of Genoa had just been cut by the capture of Ceva. After useless attempts to retake this place, he saw his only chance of safety was by throwing himself into the mountains. To obtain this end he marched all his baggage and heavier ordnance towards France by the Fenestrelle Pass; then, by opening for himself a passage by the St. Bernard, he gained Loano with his field artillery and the few equipages he had preserved. By this skilful march he preserved his communication with France, and found himself even able to watch the movements of the army of Naples, in order to facilitate his junction by bearing on the necessary points with all his assembled forces.

Macdonald, who could not hope for the success of his march but by concentrating his little army, yet neglected this precaution, and was beaten in three successive battles at the crossing of the Trebbia. Thus, by the slowness of his march, he rendered fruitless the measures of Moreau to unite the two armies on the plains of the Po, and his retreat, after brilliant but useless efforts at the passage of the Trebbia, made nugatory the dispositions Moreau had taken to come to his aid. The inaction of Marshal Savaron finally allowed the French general to effect his junction with the Neapolitan army. Concentrated on the Apennines, the French army was able to defend the important positions of Liguria till the chances of war should offer it the means of resuming the offensive.*

---

* *Events are in the saddle*, they say; and *Qui vivra verra*. I vouch for the substantial truth of the following and significant notice in view to the near future, in case of European wars. In 1873, even then Prince Napoléon (called *Jérôme*, nicknamed *Plon-Plon*, and Prince *Victor Napoléon's* father) was believed to have seen in the hands of King Victor Emmanuel (his father-in-law) a map of France recently drawn with the provinces of Franche-Comté (*Haute-*

When, after a decisive battle, an army has lost its artillery and equipages, and in consequence thereof is not in a position to resume the offensive, nor even to be able to stop the enemy's pursuit, it seems to be more advantageous to divide the remnants of the army into several divisions, which, by different directions, will march on the line of operations to throw themselves into fortresses. It is the only chance of safety, for the enemy, uncertain as to the march of the conquered army, does not know at first which division to pursue, and the moment of indecision may be used to gain a march. Besides, the movements of one small body are much easier than those of great masses, so that this divergent disposition is wholly in favour of the retreating army.

XIV.

In the campaign of 1793, in the Maritime Alps, the French Army, under General Brunet, did all that was

---

Saône, Doubs, Jura), Nice (*Alpes-Maritimes*) and Savoie (*Savoie* and *Haute-Savoie*) cut off. War was spoken of between Italy and France at that time; Italy was feeling excited and irascible, but "cocksure" Prussia was standing by near, ready to support the Italians. As war might take place, sooner than people in Europe expect, between Continental Nations, *raison de plus* for Military Students to give History their close attention, which, well read and duly understood, is the best school to fathom the endless problems of European politics and warfare to be solved. Italy is of greater importance to soldiers and sailors than to tourists who seek about that uncertain country for holiday haunts only; and who look on Rome as a quaint old farm-house swarming with preaching friars, jovial monks, stately prelates, fair dames, and haughty courtiers, all rushing after the Pope mounted on his English *automobile*. Thanks to her extended sea-coasts, Italy is a NAVAL Power as well as Military, remember. Italy's situation *en double face* along the two Mediterranean basins of the Adriatic and the Tyrrhenian Seas entitles her to the rank of a genuine Sea Power. Moreover, the Italians are taking good care to be ready for war; and they have provided themselves with a first-rate Navy. The Italian Fleet has most powerful battleships, such as the *Lepantŏ*, and the *Re Humberto*, of 6,500 tons; and no European Navy is so advantageously favoured as the Italian is with her first-class naval positions of Spezzia and Madalena; and Sicily is just the spot for a first-class *colombier militaire* and for a Balloon Establishment between Italy and Malta. (L. E. H.)

possible to capture by a front attack the camp at Ranss and Fourches; their useless efforts only served to increase the courage of the Piedmontese, and to destroy the picked Grenadiers of the republican army. The manœuvres by which Napoléon forced the enemy to evacuate these positions without fighting in 1796, suffices to show the strength of these principles, and to prove again that in war success depends as much on the genius of the leader as on the courage of his troops.

XV.

In 1645 the French Army, under Condé, was marching to the siege of Nordlingen, which Count Mercy, commander of the Bavarians, had surprised, and where he had entrenched a strong position which defended Nordlingen by covering Donauworth. In spite of the enemy's advantageous position, Condé ordered the attack. It was a terrible fight; the whole infantry of the centre and right, being in turn engaged, had been routed and dispersed, in spite of efforts of the cavalry and of the reserve, which had also been carried away in the flight. The battle was lost; Condé desperate, with no centre or right, rallied the wrecks of his battalions and bore on the left wing, where Turenne was still fighting. Such perseverance inspiring fresh spirit into the troops they broke the enemy's right; then by a change of front Turenne attacked the centre. Night protected the boldness of the Prince. An entire Bavarian division, thinking it was surprised, surrendered; and the result of this determination of the French general to obtain victory gained him the field of battle, almost all the enemy's artillery, and a great number of prisoners. The Bavarian army beat a retreat, and the day after the battle Nordlingen capitulated.

XVI.

It was thus that Marshal Villeroi, a *fin courtisan*, but an incapable General Officer, taking command of the army in Italy in the campaign 1701, had the unpardonable presumption to attack Prince Eugène, of Savoy, in his entrenched post of Chiari, on the Oglio. The French officers and Catinat, with the numbers, thought this post unattackable, yet Villeroi insisted, and the result of this petty fight was the loss of the *élite* of the French army, and it would have been greater still but for the efforts of Catinat. It was by the neglect of these same principles that in the campaign of 1644, Condé failed in all his attacks on the entrenched position of the Bavarian army. Mercy, their commander, had skilfully placed his cavalry in the plain, with Freiburg on their flank, while his infantry occupied the mountains. After useless efforts the Prince, seeing the impossibility of dislodging the foe, began to manœuvre to threaten his line of communication; but as soon as Mercy saw this, he struck his camp and returned beyond the Black Mountains.

XVII.

As an interesting study on this point we should recommend the campaign of France and Spain in 1706, under the Duke of Berwick, against the Portuguese. The two armies traversed almost the whole of Spain; they commenced the campaign at Badajoz, and after having manœuvred through the two Castilles, they ended it in the kingdom of Valencia and Murcia. The army of Berwick made 85 camps, and although the whole campaign was without general actions, it cost the enemy almost 10,000 men.

A fine campaign of manœuvres was that of Marshal Turenne against Count Montecuculli in 1675; the

Imperial army having made dispositions to cross the Rhine at Strasbourg, Turenne hurried up, and throwing a bridge over the Rhine at the village of Ottenheim, three leagues above Strasbourg, he passed the river and camped with his army at the little town of Vilslet, which he occupied. This position covered the bridge of Strasbourg, so that Turenne cut off the passage to this town of his opponent. Montecuculli, having made a movement with his whole army, appeared to wish to threaten the bridge at Ottenheim, by which the French army got its provisions from Upper Alsace. As soon as Turenne had guessed the enemy's designs, he left one detachment at Vilslet and marched full strength on the village of Ottenheim. This position, intermediate between the two bridges he wished to guard, gave him the power to support either before the enemy could carry it. Thereby he foiled his antagonist's plans. Convinced that he could make no hopeful attempt between the two bridges, Montecuculli resolved to pass the Rhine below Strasbourg, and to attain this aim he came back to his first position at Offenberg. Turenne, who followed all the movements of the Austrian army, brought back his army also to the camp of Vilslet. Yet this attempt of the enemy showed the French general the danger he had run by being too far from his bridge, and he transferred it to near Strasbourg so as not to have so large a space to cover. Montecuculli, having demanded a bridge apparatus from the magistrates of Strasbourg, marched to Scherzheim to receive them, but Turenne again frustrated him by taking up a position at Freistadt, where he occupied the isles of the Rhine and immediately had a boom constructed. In fine, Turenne, during this whole campaign, obliged the enemy to follow his initiative. By a rapid march he succeeded in cutting off Montecuculli from the town of Offenberg, when he got his provisions, and would even have prevented the Austrian general from effecting his junction with Caprara's division if a cannon-ball had not ended the life of this great man.

XVIII.

In 1653, Turenne was surprised by Condé in a position dangerous to his army. He could, by a retreat, have covered it by the Somme, which he could easily have crossed at Peronne, from which he was half-a-league distant, but fearing that the move would affect the *moral* of his army, Turenne put a bold face on it, and marched to meet the foe with very inferior forces. After a march of a league, he found an advantageous position, where he awaited the fight. It was 3 p.m.; the Spaniards tired, hesitated to attack; Turenne, in the night, having entrenched, the enemy did not think it well to risk the danger of a battle, and struck their camp.

XIX.

It is by the study of the first campaign of Napoléon in Italy that one will learn what genius and boldness can do to change the action of an army from the defensive into the offensive. The allied army, commanded by General Beaulieu, was furnished with everything to make it formidable, it was 80,000 strong, and had 200 pieces of cannon. The French army, on the other hand, counted hardly 30,000 men, with at most 30 pieces; for a long time there had been no distribution of food, bread even was not sure, the infantry was ill clad, the cavalry, ill mounted, were in a most deplorable state; all the pack-horses had died from hardship, so that the artillery service was carried on by mules; lastly there was want of pecuniary means to remedy so many ills, and such was the penury of the finances, that the Government could give but 200 louis to open the campaign. Thus the French army could not stay where it was and live, but had to advance or retreat. Knowing the advantage of surprising the enemy, at the very commencement of the campaign, by some decisive blow, Napoléon began by strengthening the *moral* of his troops. In an energetic proclamation, he showed that an obscure death threatened them, if they stayed on the defensive, that they had nothing to expect from France, but everything from victory. "There is plenty in the fertile plains of Italy," were his words; "Soldiers! will you fail in courage or fortitude?" Profiting from the moment of enthusiasm he had inspired, Napoléon concentrated to fall with all his strength on the enemy. Soon the battles of Montenote, Millesimo and Mondovi increasing the confidence the soldiers had gained from their chief, this army, a few days before, camped in rocks, and melting away through wretchedness, ambitioned the conquest of Italy. A month after the opening of the campaign, Napoléon had ended the war with the King of Sardinia, and conquered the whole Milanese. Rich cantonments soon effaced from the French soldiers' memory the misery and hardships of this rapid march, while a vigilant administration employed all the resources of the country to supply the wants of the army, and to create the necessary means to proceed to fresh triumphs.

XX.

Frederick, however, has changed his line of operation in the middle of a campaign, but he could do so, because he was manœuvring then in the centre of Germany, a country where he could abundantly supply the wants of his army in case his communication with Prussia had been cut. Turenne, in the campaign of 1648, abandoned altogether his line of communication with the allies, but, like Frederick, he too was warring in the heart of Germany. He was marching with all his forces, and by capturing Main he secured himself a Depôt on which he could base his operations. By these bold and talented moves he forced the Imperial army to abandon to him their magazines, and to go back to Austria for winter quarters.

It seems to me, however, that such examples are not to be followed, unless one knows exactly one's opponent's measure of genius, and especially if there is no fear of a rising in the country made the seat of war.

XXI.

It is especially in mountainous country, or cut up by woods and marshes, that it is important to observe this maxim, for equipages and convoys being stopped in defile, the enemy's manœuvres may easily disperse the escorts, or attack with complete success the whole army, when, by the nature of the ground, it is obliged to march in a long drawn column.

XXII.

Frederick has said, to assure oneself of the well placing of a camp, one should see if by a petty move on one's part the enemy may be forced to an important one, or if obliged to make a retrograde march, he may be forced to do so again. In defensive warfare the camps should be entrenched on the front and flanks of position occupied, and communication on the rear quite free. If there is danger of being turned, one should be prepared in advance to take a position a little further off, so as to profit by the faults which the order of march might occasion, in the divisions of the hostile army, so as to essay some attacks on his artillery or baggage.

XXIII.

This was the manœuvre of General Denny in 1798, near Rastadt. With inferior strength, he put a bold face on—*make believe*, they say at Aldershot—and maintained his position for the whole day, in spite of strenuous attacks of Archduke Charles; in the evening he effected a retreat, and took a position in the rear.

By following out this principle, General Moreau, in the same campaign, delivered battle to Berwick to secure retreat by the outlets of the Black Mountains. A few days after he gave battle at Schlinger for the same end. Placed in a good defensive position, he threatened the Archduke with turning on the offensive, while his vehicles crossed the Rhine at the bridge of Huningen, and he made the necessary preparations to retire beyond the river.

I will observe, however, that these offensive moves should be carried out in the evening, in order not to imperil oneself by engaging too early—that cannot be long sustained with success. Night and the enemy's uncertainty will serve to favour retreat, if judged necessary. But to hide a move of this kind more effectually, fires should be lit along the whole line, to deceive the enemy and prevent him seeing this retrograde move, for in retreats it is a great advantage to gain a march on one's foe.

XXIV.

In the campaign of 1645, Turenne lost the battle at Marienthal for having forgotten this maxim, for if in place of collecting his cantonments by Erbstansen he had made Mergentheim behind the Tauber his rallying point, his army would have been together sooner, whence it would have resulted that in place of 3,000 men whom Count de Mercy had to fight at Erbstansen, and of whom he gave a good account, he would have had the whole French Army to attack, in a position protected by a river.

Someone having indiscreetly asked Turenne why he had lost the battle, he replied : " By my fault, sure"; but he added, " when a man has made no faults in war, it is because he has not warred long."

XXV.

Such was the position of the French army at the battle of Leipzic, which, in a way, was so fatal to Napoléon in the campaign of 1813, for the fight at Hanau could be of no consequence in the desperate condition of his army.

It seems to me that in a position like that of the French army before the battle of Leipzic, a general should not count on lucky chances which may procure him the offensive, but that he should rather take all possible means to secure his retreat. To attain this end he must surround himself with good entrenchments, in order to withstand with inferior forces the attacks of the enemy, while the equipages of the army pass the defile. As the troops reach the other bank, they should hold a position which would protect the crossing of the rear, which would maintain itself in a *tête-de-pont* till the army should evacuate the camp. During the wars of the Revolution, too little account was made of entrenchment; thus we have seen great armies dispersed after a single check, and the fate of nations affected by the issue of one battle.

XXVI.

The battle of Hohenlinden was lost to the Austrians by the neglect of this principle. The Imperial army, under the Archduke John, was divided into four columns, who marched into an immense forest, in order to join on the plain of Anzing, where they were to surprise and attack the French. But these different divisions, which had, so to speak, no intercommunication, were compelled to engage singly an enemy who had taken the precaution to concentrate his forces, and who could move them at will over a long explored ground; thus the Austrian army, caught in the defiles of the forest with all its trains, was attacked on flank and rear, and the Archduke owed only to night the power of rallying his beaten and scattered legions. The trophies of this victory were to the French army immense—11,000 prisoners, 100 pieces of cannon, many standards, and all the baggage. The Austrians left 7,000 dead on the field.

The battle decided the fate of the campaign of 1800, the brilliant and well-merited success of which placed Moreau among the best generals of this century.

XXVII.

One great advantage which may result from rallying columns to a point distant from the field of battle, or from one's position, is the enemy's uncertainty as to the direction you will take. If he divides his forces to pursue you, he risks seeing his detachments being separated, in case you have hastened and made your junction in time enough to place yourself between his columns and disperse them one after the other.

It was by such a manœuvre that, in the campaign of 1799, in Italy, General Mêlas gained the battle of Genoa. General Championnet—the General Administrator of the "Republica Parthenopea" at Naples—commanded the French army; he sought to cut the communications of the Austrian army with Turin by setting into action bodies which manœuvred separately to attack him in the rear. Mêlas, who guessed these designs, executed a retrograde march, by which he made his adversary believe that he was in full retreat; this movement, however, had in view the concentration of his forces on the rallying points of several detachments of the French army, which he defeated and scattered one after another by his great numerical superiority. It was also by forgetting this principle that General Beaulieu, the commander of Austro-Sardinians, in the campaign of 1796, lost the battle of Millesimo after that of Montenotte. His aim, in seeming to rally his different divisions at Millesimo, was to cover the roads to Turin and Milan, but Napoléon, seeing the advantage of the enthusiasm of his troops encouraged by a former success, attacked him before he could get together his divisions, and by skilful manœuvres succeeded in separating the two armies. They retired in the greatest disorder, the one by the Milan and the other by the Turin road.

XXVIII.

In 1796, the army of Sambre and Meuse, commanded by General Jourdan, effected a retreat; the difficulty was increased by loss of its line of communications. Yet, seeing the forces of the Archduke scattered, Jourdan, to effect his retreat on Frankfort, resolved to open the way to Wurzburg, where there were but two divisions of the Austrian army. This movement would have been made successfully if the French general, who thought he had but two divisions to fight, had not committed the mistake of attacking Lefebvre's division which he left at Schweinfürth to cover the only direct communication of the army with its base. This first fault, and being a little burdened in his march, assured victory for the Archduke, who hastened to concentrate his forces; the two divisions of Kray and Wurtensleben, which arrived during the fight, made him able to oppose 50,000 men to the French army, which numbered hardly 30,000 ; it was, therefore, beaten and compelled to continue its retreat by the mountains of Fulda, where the roads are as bad as the country is difficult. Lefebvre's division, about 40,000 strong, could have restored the chances of fighting in favour of General Jourdan, but, perhaps, he thought it unadvisable to force only his way through the divisions which barred the way to Wurzburg.

XXIX.

I think that it would be useless to observe that it would be prudent to fix, behind the line of the reserves, the points where the various regiments are to come up. For—if by unforeseen causes, their detachments are not able to come up before the commencement of battle—there is no need to expose them to have to meet the main body of the enemy's troops, in case a retrograde move should be made necessary. It is as well to leave the enemy in ignorance of their reinforcements in order to deal him decisive blows. Support arriving when wanted makes the success of a battle certain, because an enemy will believe the aid to be stronger than it really is ; and will, therefore, lose courage.*

XXX.

It was for neglect of this principle that Frederick lost the battle of Kolin, in the first campaign of 1797. In spite of prodigies of valour, the Prussians lost 15,000 men and a great part of their artillery, while the loss of the Austrians only amounted to 5,000 men. The result of this battle was still more unfortunate, since the King of Prussia was forced to abandon Prague and evacuate Bohemia.

---

* *Make believe* is the expression used at Aldershot. (I., E. H.)

It was also for having made a flank march before the Prussians that the French lost the shameful battle of Rosbach. This improvident march was so much the more reprehensible because the Prince of Soubise, who commanded the French army, had pushed negligence to the point of manœuvring in presence of the enemy without having guards, van or flank ; thus, his army, 50,000 strong, was attacked by six battalions and 30 squadrons. It lost 7,000 men, 27 standards, and a large number of pieces of cannon ; the Prussians had only 300 men disabled. Thus, for having forgotten this principle : that flank marches should never be made before an army in line of battle, Frederick, at Kolin, lost his army ; and Soult, at Toulouse, his army and his honour.

XXXI.

" War should be made so as to leave nothing to chance," said Marshal Saxe, and it is in this mainly, that the skill of a general is perceptible. But when he has gone so far as to give battle, he should peg away and make short work of it all to profit by victory ; and especially, not to be content with gaining the field of battle as is the custom. It was by neglecting to pursue a first success that the Austrian army, after driving the French out of the village of Marengo and compelling Napoléon to retreat as far as St. Juliano, was compelled, on the next day, to evacuate the whole of Italy. General Mélas, seeing the French retreating, left the direction of the movements of his army to the chief of his staff, and retired from the field quite secure of the victory, and went to Alessandria to rest after the fatigues of the day. General Mélas was more than eighty years of age ; and he had been many hours on horseback. It is natural that the old General's strength should have given way ;

and the brave old man needed rest of course. Colonel Zach, not less convinced than his general that the French army were but fugitives to be pursued, formed the columns into a marching column, so that the Imperialist army awaited the order to march in a disposition not less than a mile long. It was almost four o'clock when General Desaix rejoined the French army with his division; his presence somewhat restored an equilibrium of forces. Yet Napoléon for an instant hesitated between retaking the offensive, or utilizing this division to secure his retreat; he cast a rapid glance round the troops, and spoke thus:—
" We have retired enough for to-day; you know I always sleep on the field of battle." The army, by its unanimous cry, seemed to promise him victory in advance. Napoléon resumed the offensive, and the Austrian vanguard, terror-stricken to see so formidable a mass appearing suddenly at a point where they had only seen fugitives, turned right-about and retired in disorder—the horse galloping over the Infantry—on the main body of the column; soon, impetuously attacked on its rear and flanks, the Austrian army was completely routed.

Marshal Daun suffered almost the same fate as Mêlas at the battle of Torgau, in the campaign of 1760. The position of the Austrian army was excellent, it had its left at Torgau, right on the plateau of Leiptiz, and front covered by a large pond. Frederick proposed turning his right to attack him from the rear, and for this purpose divided the Prussian army into two parts, one under Ziethen to attack in front, along the banks of the pond, and he put himself in command of the other to turn the Austrian right. But Daun, knowing of the manœuvres of his opponent, made a change of front by a countermarch, and was thus enabled to repulse Frederick's attacks, who was compelled to retreat. These two divisions of the Prussian Army had acted without connection, yet Ziethen, hearing the noise growing fainter, concluded therefrom that the king had been beaten, and he was about to make a move on his left and rejoin his master; but meeting with five battalions of the reserve, the Prussian General profited thereby to retake the offensive. He then recommenced his attack with vigour, seized the plateau of Leiptiz, and soon had possession of the whole battle-field. The sun had set when the King of Prussia was informed of his lucky event, he returned in all haste, profited by the night to re-organise the wrecks of his army, and the day after the battle occupied Torgau. Marshal Daun was receiving compliments on his victory when he heard of the return of the Prussian army; he immediately ordered retreat and at daybreak the Austrians had re-crossed the Elbe, with the loss of 12,000 men, 8,000 prisoners and 45 pieces of cannon.

After the battle of Marengo, General Mélas, although in the midst of his magazines and strong places, saw himself compelled to surrender everything to save the remnants of his army. General Mack capitulated after the battle of Ulm, although he was in his own country. The Prussians, despite their magazine and reserves, after the battle of Jena, and the French after that of Waterloo, were compelled to lay down their arms. Whence it may be concluded that after the loss of a battle the greatest evil is not the loss of men and material, but the dejection which is the result of a defeat. The courage and confidence of the victor increasing as that of the vanquished diminish, it results that, whatever be the resources of an army, a retreat will soon be changed into a rout, if the General-in-chief does not join genius to audacity, firmness to perseverance, to restore the *moral* of his army.

XXXII.

The advice of Frederick was that a vanguard should be composed of detachments of each arm of the service; its commander should know how to make a skilful choice of his camp, and that he should be informed by numerous patrols of what happens at every moment in the enemy's camp. During battle, the duty of a vanguard is not to fight, but to watch the enemy in order to cover the movements of the army. In pursuits it should charge with vigour and seek to surround the trains and isolated divisions which it pursues; moreover to attain this end, it should be reinforced by all the squadrons of light cavalry at hand.

XXXIII.

Nothing is more embarrassing on the march of an army than a quantity of baggage. In the campaign of 1796, Napoléon abandoned his siege-train before Mantua, after having spiked the cannon and broken the gun carriages; by this sacrifice, he acquired the power of manœuvring his little army with speed in order to have the initiative and be superior to the numerous, but divided, forces of Marshal Wurmser.

In 1799, during his retreat in Italy, General Moreau, having to manœuvre through the mountains, preferred to separate from his whole reserve-park, which he dispatched to France by the pass of Lenestretta, rather than to clog his march by keeping his trains. Such examples are to be followed; for if by rapidity of one's marches and the power of concentrating one's forces on decisive points, victory is obtained, the material of an army is soon replaced; if on the contrary, one is conquered and forced to retreat, it would be very difficult to save one's trains, and we should congratulate ourselves that we had the prudence to abandon them in time, since they would otherwise only have served to increase the trophies of the enemy.

XXXIV.

In the campaign of 1757 the Prince of Lorraine, who was covering Prague with the Austrian army, perceived that the Prussians were seeking to outflank his right wing and turn it. He made the Infantry execute change of front to the rear, so as to form in square on the extremity of the centre. This march being made in the presence of the enemy, did not take place without disorder. The heads of columns having marched too rapidly they stretched out, and having then formed on the right, left a great space near the salient angle. Frederick perceived this fault, and hastened to profit by it; he ordered the centre division, commanded by the Duke of Bevern, to throw himself into this space, and by this manœuvre, decided the fate of the day. The Prince, beaten and pursued, retired into Prague with the loss of 6,000 men and 200 guns.

We should remark that it does not do to throw oneself into the intervals presented by an army, except one has equal forces, and is able to outflank the foe, for then the sole hope is to assault the hostile centre, and to combat its two wings separately. But if inferior in numbers there is the risk of being barred by the reserves and crushed by the wings of the enemy, who might deploy on your flanks and overwhelm you. This manœuvre gained Marshal Berwick the battle of Almanza, in the campaign of 1707 in Spain. The Anglo-Portuguese army, under the orders of Lord Galway, had sat down before Villena; but Berwick, the Franco-Spanish commander, left his camp at Montalegre and marched to the relief of this town. At his approach, the English

General, who wished to deliver battle, advanced to meet him in the plains of Almanza. Success was long doubtful; however, the first line of the division, commanded by the Duke of Popoli, having been broken, Chevalier d'Asfield, commanding the second, disposed his masses so as to form spaces between them, and when the English, who pursued the first line, arrived on his reserves, he profited by the order in which they were, to attack them in flank, and completely defeated them. Berwick seeing the success of this manœuvre, opened the front of his line of battle, and by deploying on the enemy's flanks, with the reserves in front, and the cavalry on the rear, he obtained a complete success. Lord Galway, wounded and pursued, only rallied with difficulty the wrecks of his army, and brought them into Tortose.

XXXV.

At the battle of Dresden, in the campaign of 1813, the camp of the allies, on the left bank of the Elbe, although advantageously placed on the heights, was altogether defective, since it was cut transversely by a very steep ravine, so that the left wing was entirely isolated from the centre and the right. This vicious disposition did not escape the penetrating eye of Napoléon, who brought down all his cavalry, and two bodies of infantry on this left, attacked it by superior forces, routed it, and took 10,000 prisoners before any assistance could arrive.

XXXVI.

If one occupies a town or village on the opposite bank to the enemy, it is advantageous to choose this spot for the point of passage, because it is easier in a town than in the open country, to cover the reserves, park and trains and to hide the bridge works. It is also a great advantage to effect the passage opposite a village, when it is but feebly occupied by the foe, because, as soon as the van has landed on the other side, it may carry this post, station itself there, and by offensive works, convert it quickly into a *tête-de-pont;* one secures thus, to the remainder of the army, the power of crossing.

XXXVII.

Frederick has said that the passage of great rivers, in the face of the enemy, is one of the most delicate feats in war. Success in this case depends on the secrecy and rapidity of the moves, and on the punctual execution of the orders given to the different divisions; for to cross these obstacles, in the presence of a foe and unknown to him, not only should the dispositions be well made, but they should be carried out without confusion.

In the campaign of 1705 in Italy, Eugène wishing to support the Prince of Piedmont, sought a favourable point to force the passage of the Adda, guarded by the French army under the Duke of Vendôme. After having chosen a favourable position, he placed a battery of 20 guns on a position commanding the opposite bank, and by erection of parallel entrenchments on the slope of this eminence, he covered his infantry from the enemy's fire. They were working vigorously at the construction of the bridge, when the Duke of Vendôme appeared with his whole army. At first he wished to oppose these works, but after examining Eugène's position, he deemed it vain. He then placed his army out of the reach of the Prince's batteries by supporting his two wings on the river, so as to form an arc, whose chord was the Fulda. The Marshal, having covered the position by entrenchments and abatis, could charge the columns as they issued from the bridge, and beat them one by one. Eugène examined the position of the French, deemed it impossible to cross, and at night struck his camp, after having removed the bridge. It was by this manœuvre, that the Archduke Charles, in the campaign of 1809, made the French army retire to the Isle of Löbau, after having landed on the left bank of the Danube. The army of the Archduke was disposed almost on a circle; with his right threatened Gross Aspern; his centre, Essling; his left, Enzerndorf; his army formed a semi-circle round Essling, with the two wings resting on the Danube. Napoléon ordered an attack on the centre of Austrian line of battle, and broke it; but, after forcing their first line, suffered a check from the reserve. The bridges over the Danube had just been broken, many divisions and artillery parks were still on the right bank, and this mishap, together with the Austrian army, decided Napoléon to retreat on the Isle of Löbau. This isle, where he had constructed many field-works, admirably served the purpose of an entrenched camp.

XXXVIII.

It may be observed that this middle position should, beforehand, be examined, or, better, entrenched, for the enemy will only be able to take the offensive against the division in charge of the siege works, after he has beaten the observing army, which, sheltered by its camp, may await a favourable movement to attack on flank or rear. This army so entrenched has, moreover, the advantage of being concentrated while the enemy must make detachments if he would cover his bridge, and watch the moves of the observing army, without exposing himself to be turned or seeing his bridge threatened.

XXXIX.

Marshal Saxe, in the campaign 1741, having passed the Moldau to march against a body of 14,000 men who had just come to throw themselves into Prague, left 1,000 of infantry on this river, with orders to entrench in a height opposite the *tête-de-pont*. This precaution secured his retreat and the power of re-crossing the bridge without confusion by rallying his division between the entrenched height and the *tête*. Are such examples unknown to the generals of modern times, or have they deemed such precautions superfluous?

XL.

The brilliant successes of the allied powers, in the campaign 1814, have given many military men false ideas as to real value of strong places. The formidable masses which crossed the Rhine and Alps at this epoch permitted the formation of numerous detachments required to blockade the fortresses of the French frontier, without injuring the numerical superiority of the army marching on the capital, which army could, therefore, act without fearing that its retreat was threatened. But at no time in the history of war have the armies of all the powers of Europe been said to march combined, and animated with the same spirit to accomplish one unique result. The group of fortresses surrounding France should then play the passive part it played in this campaign. It seems to me presumption to think it possible to cross with impunity, a frontier guarded by numerous strong places, and to fight with these fortresses behind, without having previously besieged them or at least invested them with sufficient forces.

XLI.

When a place is besieged, says Montecuculli, post should not be taken opposite its weakest point, but in position most suitable for pitching the camp and carrying out the designs formed. This is also the maxim of the Duke of Berwick, sent to besiege Nice, 1686; he determined to attack it from the Mont-Alpine side, despite the advice of Vauban and of the wishes of the king himself. Having at his disposal a small army, his first duty was to secure his camp, and this he did by constructing redoubts on heights so as to bar the space between the Var and the Paillon, which river supported his flanks. He sheltered himself from surprise, for the Duke of Savoy, being able to appear suddenly through the Col di Tenda, the Marshal must have been able to get together his troops, so as to meet the enemy rapidly, and fight him before his position had been taken.

Marshal Saxe, besieging Brussels with 28,000 men only against a garrison of 12,000, received news that the Prince of Waldeck was getting together his troops to raise the siege. Not being strong enough to form an observing army, the Marshal went and prepared a battle-field on the bank of the Volnive, and he made the necessary dispositions to betake himself there rapidly in case the enemy approached. He then made ready to receive the enemy without discontinuing the siege-works.

XLII.

During the siege of Mons, 1691, the Prince of Orange assembled his army and advanced to Notre Dame de Hall with the intention of securing the place ; Louis XIV., who was directing the siege in person, summoned a council of war to consult as to what should be done in case the Prince approached. The advice of Marshal Luxembourg,[*]

---

[*] The Prince of Orange, feeling desperate at not being lucky enough to catch Marshal de Luxembourg "nappy" and to put him *hors de combat*, used to say about this stubborn foe :—" Shan't I ever be able to lick that hump-backed devil then ? "—Marshal de Luxembourg replied when told of the Prince's remark : " *Qu'en sait-il ? Il ne m'a jamais vu par derrière !*" (L. E. H.)

which was accepted, was to remain within the line of circumvallation ; his reason was that when the besieging army was not strong enough to keep the whole line of circumvallation, a sortie is to be made and the enemy attacked ; but when the army is strong enough to camp on two lines round the place, it is better to profit by a good entrenchment ; so much the more so as thereby the siege is not interrupted. In 1658, Marshal Turenne, besieging Dunkirk, had already opened the trenches, when the Spanish Army, under Don Juan, Condé, and Hocquincourt, appeared in sight and took up position on the Downs, one league distant from the besieging army. Turenne was inferior in numbers. Yet he decided to leave his lines, but the Marshal had all the advantage on his side, for the enemy had no artillery and their superiority in cavalry was of no use, since the ground was not favourable to that arm ; it was, then, important to beat the Infantry army before it had time to entrench and to receive its artillery. The success gained by the French in this battle justified Turenne's combinations.

Berwick besieging Philipsburg, 1734, had to fear that Eugène might attack him, before the end of siege, with all the forces of the Empire. After placing the troops which were to conduct the siege, the Marshal formed, with the remainder of his army, a body of observation to make head against the Prince, if he either attacked the army in his lines, or wished to make a diversion on the Moselle or Upper Rhine. Eugène presenting himself before the besieging army, some general officers did not know the enemy should be awaited in the lines, but met and attacked. However, Berwick, who thought, like Luxembourg, that an army which could throw up good entrenchments, could not be fixed, persisted in stopping in his lines. Experience proved this to have been the opinion of Eugène himself; for he did not dare to attack the entrenchment, which he would certainly have done, if he had now any hope of forcing them.

XLIII.

If your numbers are inferior do not make entrenchments behind you, for the enemy can bring all his forces either on a few points and break through them; if equal, do not do so either; if superior, there is no need. However, despite this opinion that entrenchments are useless, Marshal Saxe often made use of them. In 1797 Generals Provera and Hohenzollern, having appeared to raise the siege of Mantua, where General Wurmser was shut up, were stopped by the lines of St. George. This slight obstacle was enough to give time to Napoléon to arrive at Rivoli and to defeat their enterprise. The latter did not forget that it was through neglecting to have a line of entrenchments, that the siege had to be raised in the preceding campaign.

XLIV.

A few scattered battalions in a town inspire no fear, but when enclosed in the narrower precincts of a citadel they are imposing. This precaution, as I think, is not only necessary to fortresses, but wherever there are depôts for wounded or stores. In default of a citadel, a favourable quarter for defence should be chosen, and entrenched so as to deal with any possible resistance.

XLV.

In 1705 the French, besieged in Haguenau by Count de Thungen, saw they were unable to hold out. The Governor Ren, who had distinguished himself by a strenuous defence, not hoping to obtain a capitulation except as prisoners of war, cut his way through. In order to secure the secrecy of his design to deceive the enemy, and to try at the same time the spirit of his junior officers, Ren summoned a council of war, and announced that he had resolved to die at daybreak; then under pretext of his desperate position, he kept the whole garrison under arms, and at night leaving only a few spear holders at the breach, he ordered his garrison to march out, and leave Haguenau in silence. Success crowned this bold resolution, and Ren arrived at Saverne without the least loss. Two notable defences in modern times are those of Massena at Genoa and of Palafox at Saragossa. The first marched out with arms and baggage and all honours of war, after having rejected all summonses, and held out till famine compelled him to yield; the second only gave in after he had buried his garrison under the ruins of the town which he defended from house to house till hunger and death made it for him an absolute necessity to surrender. This last siege, as honourable to French as to Spaniards, is one of the most memorable in history of war. Palafox had shown, during this siege, all that obstinacy and courage can do to prolong the defence of a place. The true strength is in the will; thus, moreover, I think that in the choice of a Governor, less attention should be paid to his talents than to his character, for his chief qualities should be courage, perseverance and devotion; he should especially have the talent of inspiring not only the garrison, but the whole population of the place; otherwise whatever the skill displayed in multiplying defence works, the garrison will be compelled to surrender at the first or at most the second assault.

XLVI.

Marshal de Villars has said that the garrison of a place can never excuse a surrender by the desire of sparing the King's troops. No garrison which displays firmness should become prisoners of war ; for no general, assured though he may be of success, but will prefer giving a capitulation to conquering obstinacy by a thousand lives.

XLVII.

A general, says Frederick, should take care to secure the tranquillity of his cantonments in order that the soldier may rest in peace after his fatigue. To attain this end, we should observe that the troops should rapidly form on ground marked out beforehand, that the generals should be with their divisions or brigades, and that watch should be strictly kept.

Marshal Saxe is of opinion that there is no necessity to hasten to leave cantonments, but rather the general should wait till the enemy is weakened by marching before falling on him with fresh troops, while his are worn out. I think, however, it would be dangerous to take this advice as a maxim, for there are many circumstances which give an advantage to taking the initiative, especially when the enemy has been obliged to extend his cantonments, by reason of the scarcity of subsistence, and then he may be attacked before he has had time to concentrate.

XLVIII.

It seems to me, if the occasion requires, that infantry should be formed into a square. The two-deep formation will be too thin to resist the attack of cavalry. However useless a third line may appear for a march past, it is necessary in action in order to replace the men who fall in first and second rank ; otherwise it will be necessary to close ranks, and to leave between the companies intervals of which cavalry will not fail to profit. Again, when the infantry is two deep, the columns should be close to one another on flank marches.

Behind the entrenchments, if it is found more advantageous to post the infantry two-deep, the third rank should be in reserve, and this will be made use of to replace the first line, when tired, or when the firing is ceasing to be brisk. I would not venture to make these observations, but that I have read in an excellent pamphlet, "On the Infantry," the statement that the two-deep formation is the best; the author proves it, indeed, by a number of excellent reasons, but insufficient to answer all the objections that might be made.*

XLIX.

This, too, was the advice of Marshal Saxe. He says: "The weakness of this order, is, of itself, sufficient to make platoons of infantry waver, because they feel themselves lost if the cavalry is beaten; the cavalry trusting to the support of infantry, and after some rather sharp moves, no longer seeing it, will be disconcerted." Turenne and the generals of his time, have sometimes used this arrangement, but that is not sufficient to induce a modern author to represent it as advantageous in his "Considerations on the Art of War." This order is long out of date since the creation of light cavalry, and it would be absurd to propose it.

L.

Archduke Charles, speaking of cavalry, recommended massing it on the decisive point, till the moment for using it has arrived, *i.e.*, when it can attack with a certainty of success. When the briskness of its pace allows it to operate on the whole line in one day, the general-in-command should, as much as possible, get together in large masses, and not make too many detach-

---

* This has hardly any practical meaning when applied to contemporary tactics. (L. E. H.)

ments. When the nature of the ground permits it to be so employed, it is best to form it behind the infantry, in a position from which it may be able to act anywhere occasion may demand. If the cavalry is to cover a position, it should be posted behind to intercept troops coming to attack this position. If it is proposed to make it cover the flank of infantry, it should, for the same reason, be placed behind. Its use being purely offensive, a rule is to form it at a sufficient distance from the point at which it is to engage, in order that speed should be gained to give it sufficient impetus on arrival. As to the cavalry reserve, it should not be used until the end of the battle, either to make success decisive, or to protect a movement of retreat. Napoléon observes, that at the battle of Waterloo, the cavalry of the guard, which formed his reserve, was engaged against his orders; he complains of having, for five hours, been deprived of the aid of this reserve, which, well employed, had so often assured him victory.

LI.

Victor, or vanquished, it is always advantageous to have squadrons of cavalry in reserve, either to profit by victory or to secure retreat, for we have seen many decisive battles lost because the victor failed to follow up his success, and thus to prevent all chance of his opponent rallying. When a retreating army is being pursued, the cavalry must be launched on its flanks, if sufficient to cut off the line of retreat.

LII.

Light artillery is a creation of Frederick. Austria's armies soon adopted it, but in an imperfect manner. It was only adopted by France in 1792, but was then carried to its present pitch of excellence. The services it rendered during the Revolutionary Wars, were immense; and it may be said that it in some measure changed tactics, since its mobility allows it to bear rapidly on all points where artillery can insure complete success.

Napoléon has said in his memoirs that a battery which sweeps, commands, and fires on the enemy crossways, may decide the issue. Thus, besides that light artillery is necessary to secure the flanks of the cavalry, and to prepare success for a charge by a volley of grape shot, these two arms should be always together, when it is required to seize positions deemed suitable for the reception of batteries. In this case the cavalry masks the advance of the artillery, protects it while getting into position, and covers it from the enemy's attacks.

LIII.

The better the infantry the more reason its strength should be husbanded by the support of artillery. It is also necessary that the artillery attached to the divisions should march in front, because thereby the *moral* of the soldier is strengthened, who attacks with more assurance when he feels sure that the flanks of the column are covered by artillery. The reserve artillery should be employed at a decisive moment, and in a mass, because it is then difficult for the enemy to do anything against it, for there are but few examples of a battery of 60 guns being taken or silenced by a charge of cavalry or infantry, unless when unsupported, or easily turned.

LIV.

The battery of 18 guns, which covered the centre of the Russian army at the Battle of Moskowa (Borodino), may be added as an example. Its position on a rounded eminence gave it such power that it was able to render indecisive for a long time the vigorous attacks made by the French right. Twice broken, the Russian left pivoted on this battery, and twice recovered its first position. Several times attacked with rare intrepidity, this battery was at length carried by the French, though with the loss of picked troops, and Generals Montebrun and Caulaincourt. Its capture decided the retrograde march of the Russian troops. We may also cite in the campaign of 1809, the terrible effect of General Lauriston's 100 guns against the Austrian right at the battle of Wagram.

LV.

The great advantage attending the assemblage of an army in a camp, is the greater facility thereby gained for keeping up its spirit and enforcing discipline. The soldier in cantonments gives himself joyfully to repose ; in the end he becomes satisfied, and fears the return to the field. The contrary takes place in a camp, where the tedium and superior discipline makes him wish the campaign to open, so as to break the dull routine of service for the various chances which war presents. An army, besides, is more safe in camp from surprise than in cantonments, which almost always possess the weakness of occupying too great an extent of ground.

In case cantonments are necessary, General Feuquières, in his *Mémoires sur la guerre*, recommends the choice of a camp on the front of the line, and to assemble the troops there, either on a sudden to see if the watches are kept diligently, or with the sole aim of getting together the various corps.

LVI.

This seems to me more applicable to the soldiers than to officers ; for, war, not being a natural condition to man, it is necessary that those who reason as to its causes should be inspired by some passion. In order that an army should do great things in a war in which it takes no interest, it should be animated with great enthusiasm and devotion to its chief; this is sufficiently proved by the usual want of vigour in auxiliary troops when not carried away by their leader.

LVII.

This is irrefutable, especially for an army which has to fight after the system of modern wars, when success rests chiefly on the order, precision, and rapidity of the manœuvres—and on shooting especially.

LVIII.

Courage belongs as well to the recruit as to the veteran, but is of a more transient nature; it is by training, and after many campaigns that the soldier acquires the moral courage to suffer without complaint the hardships and privations of war; experience teaches him to supply himself with what he wants; he contents himself with what he can procure, because he knows success is only to be obtained by persistent effort. Napoléon could well say that misery is the soldier's school, for nothing can be compared to the destitution of the Army of the Alps when he assumed the command; as also nothing to the brilliant success he achieved with this same army in his first Italian campaign. The troops which conquered at Montenotte, &c., had seen, a few months before, whole rag-clad battalions desert for want of victuals.

LIX.

It is fortunate that Napoléon has recognised the advantage of providing the soldier with pioneering tools; for his authority will combat the ridicule sought to be thrown on those who have proposed it. A hatchet will not trouble the soldier more than the useless sabre he wears at his side, and will be much more useful. Those which are divided among each company, and in the field carried by camp followers, do not fail to be lost; thus when it is required to camp it is very difficult to cut wood and erect huts, for want of the necessary instruments. On the other hand, by making the hatchet an integral part in the armament of the soldier, he will be obliged to have it always with him, and whether he wishes to entrench in a village, or to establish huts in a camp, a division commander will not fail to observe the advantage to be gained by this innovation. The hatchet once adopted, it will perhaps also be deemed necessary to give pickaxes and shovels to certain companies and to entrench more often.

It is in retreats especially that it is important to entrench, when a good position has been obtained, for an entrenched camp not only gives a pursued army increased power of rallying, but also if it is so fortified as to appear to the enemy unable to be successfully attacked, the fact will not fail to strengthen the *moral* of the retreating troops, and to give the general-in-chief means of resuming the offensive, in profiting by the first vicious dispositions he sees taken by his adversary. We know that in the campaign of 1761, Frederick, surrounded by the two Russian and Austrian Armies, whose conjoined forces were four times the number of his, yet saved his army by entrenching at the camp of Bunzelwitz.

LX.

Some modern writers, on the contrary, have proposed to shorten the duration of service, in order to bring in turn all young men under the standards; they claim thereby that they obtain mass levies, quite well trained, and capable of repelling with success an invasion. However brilliant at first sight such a system of military forces may appear, I think its advantages may easily be gainsaid, for the soldier, tired by the minute garrison service and the yoke of discipline, will not be very anxious to go through it again, after he has received his discharge, and so much the more because having served the prescribed time, he will think he has fulfilled the duties every citizen owes to his country; he returns home, marries, takes up some trade, rapidly loses the military spirit, and soon becomes unfit for war. On the other hand, the soldier who serves a long time becomes attached to his regiment as to a new family; he forgets the yoke of discipline, accustoms himself to the privations his state imposes, and at last he actually likes his situation. There are few officers who have been engaged in war who do not know the difference between young and old soldiers, either to support the fatigue of a long campaign, or to attack with true courage, or finally to rally after having been driven back in disorder.

Montecuculli has said that time is necessary to discipline an army, still more so to inure it to war, and more so to make good troops; he also recommends that special attention should be paid to veteran warriors, special care taken of them, and a fair number of them kept on foot.

It seems to me, then, it is not sufficient to increase a soldier's pay by reason of his years of service, but that a mark of distinction should be conferred on him which should secure him privileges, sufficient to encourage him to grow old under the standards, and to grow old with honour.

LXI.

The thought of the commander expressed with verve, has a great influence over the soldier's *moral*. In 1703, at the attack of Hornbek, de Villars, seeing the half-hearted march of the troops, hurried up in front and said: "What, shall I, a Marshal of France, be the first to mount the escalade, if I order an attack?" These few words re-awakened their courage, officers and men darted emulously on the ramparts, and the town was assaulted without loss.

"We have retreated enough for to-day; you know I always sleep on the battle-field," said Napoléon, surveying his lines at the moment he was about to resume the offensive at the battle of Marengo. These few words were enough to stir anew the courage of the soldiers, and to make them forget the fatigue of a day, during which almost all the troops had already fought.

LXII.

The acknowledged advantage of bivouacking is another reason for adding pioneers' tools to the armament of the soldier, because, by means of the hatchet and shovel, he can easily build a hut; I have seen huts made with branches of trees and covered with turf, where perfect shelter was obtained against rain and cold, even in the worst seasons.

LXIII.

Montecuculli sagely remarked that prisoners should be questioned separately in order to find, by the comparison, if they have any intention of giving false reports. The general information obtained from officers-prisoners should especially give the resources and sometimes details as to localities. Frederick advises that prisoners should be threatened by being run through, if an intention is displayed of deceiving.

LXIV.

Success, says Archduke Charles, is only obtained by simultaneous efforts, energetic resolutions, and great swiftness of execution. It is rare that many men, who wish to attain the same *meum* without the *tuum*, should be perfectly agreed as to the means, and if the will of one does not prevail, they will fail together in their operations, and will not attain the wished-for goal. It is useless to support this maxim by examples, which are but too often found in history. Eugène and Marlborough would not, perhaps, have been so fortunate in their campaigns, if intrigue and difference of opinion had not constantly disorganised the armies opposed to them.

LXV.

Prince Eugène used to say that councils of war are of no use except when an excuse is wanted for doing nothing. This is also the opinion of de Villars. A commander should then avoid calling together such a council at a perilous crisis, and confine himself to consulting separately his most experienced general officers in order to know their opinion and to decide afterwards according to his own views. He becomes then responsible for the decision he makes; but has the advantage of acting after his own conviction, and is sure that the secret of his operations will not be divulged as is usually done when they are discussed in a council of war.

LXVI.

The man who obeys, whatever be the command entrusted to him, will always be covered from his faults if he has executed orders given him. It is not the same with the general-in-chief, on whom rests the safety of the army and the success of the campaign. Incessantly busied in observing, meditating and foreseeing, it may easily be thought that he should acquire solid judgment, which will give him a grasp of things more extensive and true than that of his generals. Villars, in all his campaigns, always acted contrary to the advice of his generals. So reasonable it is that a general who feels within himself power to command an army should follow his own inspirations if he would attain success.

LXVII.

In the campaign of 1750, General Fink was detached with 18,000 men to Maxan, to cut off the defiles of Bohemia from the Austrian army. Cut off himself by double his forces, after a very stiff fight he capitulated, and 14,000 men laid down their arms. The defection was so much the more shameful as General Wunch, who commanded the cavalry, having cut his way through, the whole blame fell on General Fink, who was afterwards brought before a court-martial, dismissed from his military dignities, and condemned to 10 years' imprisonment. In the Italian campaign of 1796, the Austrian general Provera, capitulated with 2,000 men at the Castle of Grossaria, and later, at the battle of Favorite Castle, near Mantua, the same general capitulated with a body of more than 6,000 men. We dare hardly cite the shameful capitulation of General Mack, at Ulm in 1805, by reason of which some 30,000 Austrians laid down their arms; while in the Revolution wars we have seen so many generals cut their way through, with but few battalions, but with determined courage.*

---

* We were told that the Duke de Grammont, who, it will be remembered, was Foreign Secretary of France during the last days of the Empire in 1870, was anxious to let the wide world know that Prince Bismarck had resolved on fighting *in any case*. How different the military colleagues of the Imperial Duke have behaved! And their own Imperial master, as their example, slinking away from Metz on August 14th, 1870, and surrendering at Sedan

LXVIII.

The soldiers, ignorant almost always of the designs of their commander, cannot be responsible for his conduct; if he orders them to lay down their arms they must do so, unless they are wanting in that discipline which is necessary to an army of thousands of men. It seems to me that in such cases the leaders alone are responsible, and should be made to suffer the punishment due to their cowardice; for there is no instance of soldiers failing in their duty at a desperate crisis, when led by courageous and determined officers.

LXIX.

There is always plenty of time to surrender, so it should not be thought of till the last moment. I will allow myself to cite here an example of rare courage in defence, and certified by eye-witnesses. A captain of grenadiers, Dubreuil, of the 37th regiment of the line,

his 80,000 men, 2,300 officers, 10,000 horses, and 650 guns!! As to Bazaine and Bourbaki:—1st: *Bourbaki*—It has oozed out that the committee which recommends a court-martial upon Marshal Bazaine has severely blamed General Bourbaki for leaving Metz to go to Chiselhurst. It may be true that he was imposed upon by a messenger who pretended to be sent by the Empress; but even if the message had been a genuine one, the desire of the Empress to see him was no excuse for his deserting his command in the face of the enemy. 2nd—History tells us of the French heroes who had to capitulate at Toul, Strasbourg, Phalsbourg, Bitcke, Verdun, and Belfort. But the capitulation of Metz was the crushing blow: 173,000 men, 1,665 guns, 278,289 rifles, an enormous amount of ammunition, and the Regimental Colours were given up by Bazaine, who is the first Marshal of France arraigned on a charge of bad conduct in the face of the enemy. He was *nem. con.* found guilty at the court-martial held on October 6th, 1873, of which the President was H.R.H. the late Duke d'Aumale; sentenced to be shot (December 10th, 1873), he was spared death by Marshal MacMahon, President of the French Republic at that time, and sent to *Sainte-Marguerite* Island (one of the Lérins Islands on the Alpes—Maritimes Coast) as a prisoner, from whence he escaped during the night of August 9th, 1874. Born, 1811; died, 1888, abroad. The history of trials of different marshals of France who have been called on to answer for their acts since the office was first instituted by Francis I. is hardly of a nature to having been included with his company in a detachment, was stopped in his march by a large body of Cossacks, who surrounded him on all sides. He formed his little troop into a square, and sought to gain the border of a wood at some musket shots' distance from the place where they had been attacked. They arrived at one musket shot distance with but little loss; but as soon as the grenadiers saw that they could obtain almost safe refuge, they left the lines and fled into the wood, leaving their captain and brave men who would not leave him, to the mercy of the cavalry. Rallying in the depth of the wood, the grenadiers, ashamed of having deserted their captain, courageously resolved to snatch him from the enemy, if he had been taken prisoner, or at least carry off his corpse if he had succumbed. After having formed on the border of the wood, they cut their way with bayonets through the cavalry to their captain, who,

---

console Marshal Bazaine. Only five marshals of France have been tried for their lives by regular tribunals, and all five were found guilty and executed. Marshal de Retz, who was the first holder of the highest military dignity in France, was brought to trial for high treason, or rather for repeated acts of rebellion against the authority of his liege lord, John VI., Duke of Brittany. Found guilty not only of the crime with which he was originally charged, but of others still more heinous, the marshal was hanged and his body burned in 1440. The next offender was Marshal Biron, the friend and companion in arms of Henry IV. In spite of all the favours heaped on him by his Royal master, Marshal Biron was found guilty of conspiracy with the King of Spain against the first of the Bourbons. Henry IV. would have pardoned him if he would have confessed his crimes; but on his refusal to admit his guilt the King allowed sentence to be carried out, and Marshal Biron was decapitated on the Place de Grève in 1602. Marshal de Marcillac, who was executed in 1632 for conspiracy and rebellion against Cardinal Richelieu, was the third marshal of France who perished on the scaffold. Marshal de Montmorency, who was executed in the same year on a similar charge, was another of the victims of the cardinal. The last of the marshals of France who have undergone capital sentence was the best known and most celebrated of them all, Marshal Ney, shot on the 7th of December, 1815, for fidelity to his old and treachery to his new master. (L. E. H.)

despite 17 wounds, still held out; they surround him and regain the wood without much loss. Such examples are not rare in the Revolutionary wars. It is to be wished that they had been chronicled by contemporaries to teach soldiers what can be obtained in war by energetic will and resolution.

LXX.

Among the Romans, generals did not attain to the command of armies until they had passed through the different offices of the magistracy. Thus, by their administrative knowledge, generals were able to govern conquered provinces with the judgment needed by newly acquired power, supported by arbitrary force. Now-a-days, after modern military institutions, generals—versed only in what concerns strategy and tactics—are obliged to confide the administrative portion of the war to employés. This observation, which I am but repeating, yet seems to me worthy of particular attention; for if in leisure time of peace, superior officers were employed diplomatically, in the different legations of the Sovereign to foreign courts, they would learn the laws and constitutions of the various governments, whither they might one day carry the theatre of war. They will also learn to distinguish the interests which are to be consulted in the treaties which will advantageously terminate a campaign. By the aid of this knowledge a commander will obtain more sure and positive success, since all the means of war will be in his hands. We have seen Eugène and Villars filling with like skill the duty of the commander and that of the negotiator.

When the army occupying a conquered province keeps well in discipline, there are few examples of the provincials rising unless sedition is provoked by exactions of those employed in the administration, which is but too often the case. It is then principally to that the commander should turn his attention, in order to insist that the contributions should be divided justly, and especially that they should be employed to their true purpose instead of, as usually happens, enriching the employés.

LXXI.

Ambitious men, who, obeying their passions, arm citizens against one another under the deceptive veil of the public interest, seem to me still more guilty; for whatever may be the despotism of government, its institutions consolidated by time, are always preferable to civil war, and to the anarchical laws that are necessitated to justify the crimes, which are its natural consequence. To be faithful to one's Sovereign and to respect the established government, such are the qualities befitting a warrior.

LXXII.

In the campaign of 1706, Prince Eugène had the courier detained, who brought orders from the Emperor to forbid him to risk a battle. He had foreseen everything, on the other hand, to make it a decisive victory; he thought it his duty to elude the Emperor's orders, and the victory of Zanta, in which the Turks lost about 30,000 men and 4,000 prisoners, was the success which crowned his audacity. However, despite the immense advantage this victory procured to the Imperial army, Eugène was disgraced on arriving at Vienna. In 1793, General Hoche, having received orders to march on Treves, with an army worn by continual marches, in the midst of a mountainous and difficult country, he observed rightly, to gain an insignificant place, he would risk the loss of his army. He ordered his troops back to winter quarters and preferred the safety of his army, on which depended the success of the following campaign, to his own; for summoned to Paris, he was thrown into a dungeon, from which he did not issue till after the fall of Robespierre. I will not dare to decide if such examples are to be followed; it would be desirable, if this question, which appears to be a novel and very important one, were discussed by men capable of clearing it up.

LXXIII.

The first quality of a commander is a personal knowledge of war; this is acquired by experience, and is not natural; for a captain is not born, but made. Not to worry, to have an open mind, to show no change in countenance, to give orders in the midst of fight with as much coolness as when perfectly at rest, are the tests of worth in a general. To exhort the timid, to augment the small number of the brave, to stir up the fight when it grows slack, to rally the troops when broken, to bring back fortune at a desperate crisis, to give one's life if necessary to save the state, are actions pre-eminently suitable to the warrior.

To the above qualities we should add the talent of picking out men and of employing each at the post to which his character calls him. "My great attention," says Marshal de Villars, "was given to knowing the character of my junior general officers. This one, by his boldness of spirit, was suited to lead an attacking column, that one, because the natural bend of his mind was rather to caution, without however wanting in courage, would more easily defend a country." It is only by applying such knowledge at the proper season that we can obtain, and almost make certain, great success.

LXXIV.

Formerly the duties of a Chief of the Staff were limited to preparation of everything connected with the plans of campaign and operations resolved on by the commander-in-chief; in a battle he was only employed for the transmission of orders to move, and to see the movement performed. But, in the last wars, the officers of the Staff were often charged with the command of attacking columns, or of large detachments, when the general-in-chief feared to destroy secrecy by transmission of orders and instructions. Great advantages have attended this long-resisted innovation, since thereby the officers perfect theory by practice and also acquire the esteem of the soldiers and junior officers, who are prone to misjudge superior officers whom they have never seen fighting. Generals who have been successfully employed in the difficult post of Chief-of-the-Staff during the Revolutionary Wars, have nearly always kept themselves up to the work of the different branches.

Marshal Berthier, who filled so brilliantly the post of Chief-of-the-Staff to Napoléon, possessed the qualities most essential to a general: a courage cool though dashing, excellent judgment and long experience. He was in active service for more than half a century, made war in four quarters of the globe, opened and concluded 32 campaigns. In his childhood, he acquired under his father, the talent of designing and tastefully drawing plans, besides the training necessary for a Staff Officer. Admitted by the Prince de Lambesc into his regiment of dragoons, he acquired the advantage so essential to a soldier, of perfect horsemanship. Attached afterwards to the Staff of Comte de Rochambeau, commanding the French troops sent out to the help of the United States, he served his first campaign in America, where he began to be distinguished for his activity, valour, and talents. Becoming a superior officer of the Staff formed by Marshal de Ségur he visited the camps of the King of Prussia, and filled, in 1789, the duties of Chief of Staff to Baron de Besenval. For 19 years, crowned with 16 campaigns, the history of the life of Marshal Berthier is but that of the wars of Napoléon, all the details of which he carried into execution, either in the cabinet or in the field. A stranger to political intrigues, he worked with indefatigable activity, seized promptly and wisely the general view, and finally gave all orders with foresight, clearness, and conciseness. Discreet, impenetrable, modest, he was exacting, just, and severe in all that touched the service; but he always himself furnished an example of zeal and obedience, and knew how to maintain discipline, and make respected by all his subordinates, whatever their rank, the authority confided in him.

LXXV.

After having recognised the advantage of charging a military body with the task of providing arms and ammunition, it seems to me the task of providing arms and ammunition should be given to a body altogether military, and not be given to a separate administration as has been done up to now. These latter, almost always formed at the commencement of war, are composed of civilians, strangers to the laws of discipline, which they will not observe; they are but little thought of by the soldier, since they only serve to enrich one another by whatever means; lastly, they only feel for their private interest in a service to which they do not acquire glory, although a part of its success often depends upon their zeal. The disorder and waste incident to civil administration would surely cease if the post were confided to men sprung from the army, and who, as their reward for succeeding, will share with their companions in arms the glory of success.

LXXVI.

Foraging parties made with small detachments, and usually confided to young officers, was formerly the school for good officers of the outposts ; but now that the provisions of an army are got by regular contributions, it is only in partizan warfare that one can acquire the experience necessary to fill this post with success. A partizan chief is in some measure independent of the army from which he receives neither provisions nor pay, and very often none or but very small assistance, and during the whole campaign he is left to get anything he can procure. He should join stratagem to courage, prudence to boldness, if he would collect booty without exposing his little troop to combat superior forces. Always restless, always surrounded by dangers which he is to foresee and surmount, the partizan chief acquires, in a short time, experience in the details of war rarely obtained by an officer of the line ; because this latter is almost always under the influence of a superior to direct all his movements.

LXXVII.

"A man does not become a great commander without long experience and a passion for the study of war," are the words of the Archduke Charles. What a man has seen himself is not enough, for what life of man is so fertile in events as to give an universal experience ? It is then by adding to one's own knowledge from the stores of others, by justly prizing the researches of those who have gone before us, and by taking as an example the military exploits and important events with which the history of war furnishes us, that we can become great generals.

LXXVIII. & LXXIX.

It is in some measure to facilitate this study that I have drawn up this treatise. It is after a careful reading and thinking over the history of modern wars that I have striven to show by examples how to apply the maxims of a celebrated general. Would that I might have attained my aim!

LXXX.

The cavalry, needing more trained officers than the infantry, should be better trained for the van as well as the rear, and do nothing but manœuvre; it pursues or retires in square formation, it forms many lines or bends into a column, it effects a change of front with rapidity to outflank a whole wing. It is then by a combination of all these movements that a cavalry general of the van or rear, when inferior in number, should avoid too sharp actions or a general engagement, and yet delay the enemy enough to allow time to the army to arrive, to the infantry to deploy, to the general-in-chief to make his dispositions, to the baggage and artillery park to come up.

In 1796 the army in Italy was brilliantly commanded by General Van Fengel (killed at Montenotte) two or three days before his death, having preceded Napoléon by a few hours only, yet the latter, on his arrival, found everything ready. The defiles and fords had been examined, guides secured, the priest and postmaster interrogated, communication already assured with the inhabitants, spies sent in different directions, the letters seized, and those which could give military information translated and analysed; in fine all measures taken to form provision magazines to refresh the troops.

LXXXI.

There are two things required in a general: mind and character. Mind—for without it there is no power of combination, but purposeless drifting. Character—for without a will, strong and constant, the execution of the plans conceived cannot be thought of; but here relative qualities should prevail over absolute ones, and mind over character. Therein is the element of success. When the character controls the mind, and the mind has sufficient capacity, we proceed to a definite end, and have some chance of reaching it. When one has more mind than character there is a ceaseless change of opinions, designs, and direction, because a man of vast mind at every moment sees things in a new light. If the strength of his will cannot shelter a man from those changes he is always floating between different courses and adopts none definitely, and in place of bringing us nearer the goal, an uncertain march takes us much further astray. Both qualities are needed in a Commander.

So, if a general possesses a mind to see, judge and combine, and resolution to execute; when to these qualities he joins the knowledge of men, of the passions which sway them, of the secret movements of their hearts, which need so many agents to fit them for war; when besides, danger—instead of obscuring his faculties—increases and strengthens them; when, lastly, he loves his troops, is loved by them, cares for their safety, interests and well-being, then he possesses the qualities promising success.

LXXXII.

It is necessary—we think—that a commander should possess a passion for the great and the beautiful. He should be animated by every generous sentiment. A man of cold and unelevated nature will never do anything grand in the noble profession of arms. This high rank demands, too, a warm heart, a soul of fire, mastered by a cool head. As Napoléon has said: there must be a perfect equilibrium between the mind, the courage and character; with all that, if to natural genius you add the fundamental principles of the sciences; if, finally, there are favourable circumstances, then there appears on the stage of the world one of those prodigies of rareness and brilliancy. Such was Napoléon. Thence arose the enormous distance which existed between him and other modern generals. A master of the sublime parts of war, deeply versed in all its details, he possessed a soul, not as is erroneously thought, cold and insensible. Woe to those who could approach him and yet could not read into that ardent soul. There was the seat of the sacred fire he sent forth to the masses. Better than any soldier could he stir passions by a word, by a look; he could maintain and direct the enthusiasm of armies by his model orders of the day. With a thorough command over the heart and the mind, he could at will increase the exertions of the soldiers, according to the necessity and the resistance. No one ever gained such an ascendance over troops, whether belonging to his own country, to foreigners, and even to enemies. No one could, like him, found and maintain discipline worthy of the French name, which had honour for its principle, and glory for its reward.

LXXXIII.

Study the campaign of 1796-7, and you will see that it was by following this principle that Napoléon, by his skilled and bold marches, defeated in turn three armies far superior to his, and made up for numbers by the rapidity of the marches, for artillery by his manœuvres, for cavalry by his positions; thus would he exact from victory all its possible results. These two campaigns unite exactitude of calculation and a profound knowledge of men and things.

LXXXIV.

In the campaign of 1796, Moreau, general of the army of the Rhine, was so little versed in superior tactical knowledge that his irresolutions lost him precious time in two circumstances of this campaign, when he was far superior, and could easily have defeated his enemy.

On the 11th August, after the battle of Neresheim, he crossed to the right of the Danube and Lech, while by marching before him on the Altmuhl, by the left bank of the Danube, he would have in three marches joined the army of Sambre and Meuse, which was on the Rednitz, and would thereby have decided the fate of the campaign.

He remained inactive six weeks during August and September in Bavaria, while the Archduke Charles was beating the army of the Sambre and Meuse and driving it beyond the Rhine. He let Kehl be besieged for six weeks by an inferior army in sight of his, and he allowed it to be taken.

His retreat, instead of being a proof of talent, was the greatest fault he could have committed. If, instead of retiring, he had turned the enemy, he would probably have crushed or taken the Austrian army.

This same general—an excellent soldier, personally brave, and who successfully led on the field of battle at Hohenlinden — showed, in 1799, in Italy, much indecision by his want of system and ignorance of the secrets of the art of war. During the campaign of 1808, in Germany, his army, more numerous than that of the Archduke John, almost always proved inferior to him on the field of battle. This is what usually happens to generals who are irresolute and act without principles or plans, and shuffling, lose everything in war.

LXXXV.

Napoléon, who was one of the best engineer officers in his army, displayed after the battle of Essling, all the extent of knowledge necessary to an engineer to subdue bold-pushed events and elements, and the orders he gave in 1809 to utilize the fortifications of Vienna, deserve the study and attention of officers of the special branches.

LXXXVI.

The qualities necessary to a cavalry general are so varied, and so rarely found in the same man, that they seem to exclude one another.

Firstly, it requires a pure and keen eye, rapid and energetic action, but not to the exclusion of prudence; for one error, one fault, committed at the beginning of a movement is irreparable by reason of the short time required to execute it. The cavalry general should take care to shelter his men from the enemy's fire, while they are only in position, but not to spare them when the moment for the assault has come. On the eve of the battle, and till the fight is actually engaged, he should bestow on his men and horses the most minute care, and keep them up to their full strength; but when the moment has come, he should use the cavalry without the smallest regard, but with the sole object of getting as much out of them as possible.

A general of the vanguard should be energetic and fiery, while the rear general joins prudence and circumspection to vigour.

LXXXVII.

At the capitulation of Baylen in 1808, there was a circumstance as strange as in that of Maxan. General Vedel, with his division and that of General Gobert, had got a good way from the battle-field, and had his rear open to effect his retreat without much danger. One of the conditions of capitulating was that he should return to the camp and lay down his arms. This general was simple enough to obey the order given by General Dupont de L'Étang. On this point Napoléon thus expresses himself:—" That an army is beaten matters little, the fortune of war is only for the day, and defeat can be repaired; but that an army should make a shameful capitulation, is a stain to the French name, to the glory of arms. The wounds suffered by honour are never healed; they produce a terrible effect. They say there was no other means of saving the army, of preventing the slaughter of the troops. Ah! it were better they had all perished, sword in hand, that not one had returned. They would have died gloriously and we would have avenged them; soldiers may be got again, but not honour."—What about *Sedan* and *Metz* then? Napoléon III. and Bazaine!

LXXXVIII.

The light cavalry ought to reconnoitre far in front of the army; it ought to be supported and protected specially by the cavalry of the line.

Turenne, Eugène, Vendôme, and Napoléon attached great importance to dragoons as cavalry of the line. This arm was covered with glory in Italy in 1796-7. In 1813-4 the dragoons vied advantageously with cuirassiers. A division of 2,000 dragoons, moving rapidly on a point, with 1,500 light cavalry, may dismount to defend a bridge, the head of a defile, or height, and await the arrival of infantry.

LXXXIX. & XC.

A general who would wait to the end of a battle to bring his cavalry into play would give up for ever the chance of victory, and the cavalry would then be employed to cover his retreat. By so acting he would prove that he had the falsest notions on the art of war.

XCI.

Napoléon has adopted this proportion in all his campaigns; the topography of the countries in which he has made war having demonstrated its importance. The proportions of the three arms having been in all time the subject of meditation to great generals, they have agreed that this same proportion is necessary for cavalry and for artillery:—four pieces to 1,000 men.

XCII.

At Austerlitz, as at Wagram, it was in the thick of the fight that Napoléon had prepared this bronze barrier which gave him victory. In this last battle General Droust displayed the greatest intrepidity at the head of the artillery of the Imperial guard, the charge of which decided the fate of the day.

XCIII.

There is no infantry so good that it can with impunity march 1,000 or 1,200 metres against 16 well-placed guns, served by good gunners. Before three-quarters of the way the men would be killed, wounded, and dispersed.

XCIV.

In the campaign of 1757 the Prince of Lorraine, after taking Schweidnitz on 11th November, resolved to attack the Duke of Bevern in his entrenched camp in front of Breslau. The right of this camp was supported on the Oder, and the left on the village of Kleinenberg on a fine fortified plateau. The prince took up a parallel position and established himself on it. On 22nd the Austrian army seized the position of Kleinenberg and drove back the Prussians on to the valley of Breslau, which they abandoned to the conquerors with a loss of 16,000 men. The loss of this battle was due to two faults committed by the Prussian general: firstly, his position did not cover Breslau; and secondly, he had no interest in delivering battle, since he awaited the king with reinforcements. The only thing, therefore, was to guard a camp covering Breslau; and it is not easy to see how he did not attain this end, having had nearly two months to choose and fortify this camp.

XCV.

The genius of war lies in the power of rightly applying the knowledge needed for command of armies, to turn to better designs in the midst of dangerous crises. It is incomplete, if the general does not also have the knowledge of the human heart, if he has not an instinct for what is passing in the minds of his soldiers and in the enemy's camp. The various principles form the moral factor in war which mysteriously gives a spontaneous power to an army, and makes one man worth ten, and ten only worth one. There are two other faculties equally necessary, authority and decision, which are natural gifts.

However, if for a great general much intelligence is necessary, there is more character required. This it is which executes designs; which, both in ancient and modern times, has been the most dazzling mark of the first rate generals, and among them of Napoléon—

that hero, in an age fertile of heroes, versed in the mysteries of his art, but not less great in execution, prompt, indefatigable, always ready with new resources, and of the highest qualities of mind.

XCVI.

In a battle a general should oblige each one to expend all the energy he possesses, but exhaustion does come, and it is then, at this moment, so important to note that succour is imperatively demanded. For this it is necessary to employ the reserves; there is the genius of war. They must be applied with care, neither too soon nor too late; not too soon, for that is to misuse one's means, and to be in want of them when most required; nor too late, for that makes a victory indecisive, or turns a defeat into a headlong and irreparable rout. At Moskoaw or Borodino, Napoléon displayed fatal caution in refusing to bring up his guard when General Behard came to ask him at two o'clock. The Russian Army was beaten in the greatest confusion, immense results would have been secured by fresh troops; an hour's respite saves the army.

XCVII. & XCVIII.

In 1652 at the battle of Bléneau, Turenne, who had but 4,000 men, having learnt that Condé had surprised many cantonments of Marshal d'Hocquincourt, got his men together, and betook himself by a night march to Bleneau. His army and that of Condé, 12,000 men strong, did not see that they had marched past one another in opposite directions. At daylight they discovered one another. To keep in check an army three times his own till the arrival of that of d'Hocquincourt, which did not rejoin him till evening, Turenne took up position at the lake of La Roassinier. There was a defile formed by the lake on the left, and by a wood on the right. He placed his troops behind this defile, and a battery to fire on the centre, but did not occupy the wood for fear of being compelled to engage, and passed the defile with six squadrons. As soon as Condé's army approached he repassed the defile. The latter, surprised at finding his opponent in position, deployed and seized the wood, yet he appeared undecided; finally he entered the defile. Turenne then made a right-about turn with his cavalry, came down on the enemy's column before it could deploy. At that very moment he unmasked his battery which carried disorder into Condé's ranks, repassed the defile and took up position.

This manœuvre, though delicate and carried out with skill and prudence, cannot, however, be recommended. Turenne, as soon as he had got his cavalry together, had to retire on the side of St. Fargeau, but only after a junction with d'Hocquincourt. In this case, if Condé had not been wanting in boldness, Turenne would have been defeated.

XCIX.

In the campaign of 1794 in Italy, in Piedmont, Saorgio, stocked with provisions and ammunitions of all kinds, the principal depôt of the whole Piedmontese army, was surrendered to the French by the commander, although he could and should have held out for 15 days. He had been demoralized by the sudden appearance of the French army, which, by a bold manœuvre, cut off his communications.*

* To those who take an intelligent interest in the near future of Europe and in what "Military" Italy can do, we recommend the study of the admirable book *Military Italy*, written by Charles Martel (the *nom-de-plume* of an intelligent English Officer and one of my students at the Staff College), and published by Messrs. Macmillan. This book provides plenty of interest and information for the civilian as well as for the military reader and valuable food for reflection. (L. E. H.)

Fine examples of defences are that of Fort de Grave, 1678; Lille, 1708, by Boufflers; of Genoa, by Massena; of Saragossa, in 1710, by Palafox; of Burgos, in 1812, by Dalreser, and that of St. Sebastian, by Rey, in 1813. Young officers should study the decree of Napoléon of 24th December, 1811, relative to the defence of fortresses, and which displays such a great knowledge of the human heart and of the profession of arms.

C.

From the fact that the laws and customs of all nations have been specially authorised to stipulate for their interests and surrender, and that they have never authorised a general to command his troops to lay down their arms in another case, we may infer that no prince, republic, or military law, has authorised them to do so. The Sovereign or the country commands the obedience of inferior officers to their general and superior, for that is conformable to reason and to the honour of the service. Arms are placed in a soldier's hand for him to defend himself till death.

A general has received orders to employ his troops for the defence of his country, how can he have authority to order them to deliver up their arms and receive chains?*

* For that reason every French soldier curls up his lip at the very name of Napoléon III., who capitulated at Sedan as — "*N'ayant pas eu le bonheur d'être tué sur le champ de bataille !*" This the Imperial Commander-in-Chief wrote of himself to his German foes, who must have rigadooned round their mess-room in a plump fit of laughter at *Badinguet's* pitiable cheek! On this woeful day France should have taken to the Black Flag as her national standard, as the Swedes did after the death of Gustavus Adolphus, as a sign of national mourning. I am a Lorrainer; and I remember my military friends of Sedan telling me how, on the day before the battle, Napoleon III., in the streets of Sedan, leaning on his stick and walking arm-in-arm with his Aide-de-Camp, was saluted by the troops no longer! *Quel signe*! But Foreign Opinion now has a right to and does demand of France a higher perfection from an international point of view; and it might say *Pauvre peuple français !* but simplify matters by boycotting French Republicans. (L. E. H.)

CI.

The campaign of 1796, in Italy, presents models of all kinds. Offensive action skilfully and boldly carried out, defence in which inferior forces have continually beaten superior ones, while, nevertheless, oftentimes keeping the large number of men for time of action ; a war, which by its skill in direction and vigour in execution has secured a series of unexampled victories. Immortal epoch ! whose wonders have surpassed all that has ever been done before or since, for in a series of protracted fights in the midst of so many different movements, it is impossible to discover one single fault, a single forgetting of the true principles of art.

Never was an offensive or defensive war so perfect, so admirable. It is art carried into practice in its sublimest form. With moderate means immense results have been obtained.

CII. & CIII.

In the campaign of 1760, in Silesia, the great Frederick, having failed to restore his communications with Breslau, Schweidnitz and Landshut, found himself in a critical position, surrounded on all sides by forces three times his own. In the evening, 14th August, he departed from Leignitz, in the direction of Glogau. At three o'clock in the morning, as he was about to take up a position on the heights of Pfaffendorf, his main body were attacked by Landon, who, after two hours' fighting, was completely defeated. Marshal Daun had resolved this same day to deliver battle to Frederick, and had ordered Landon to pass the Katzbach on the night of the 14th or 15th, to seize the heights of Leignitz, at the same time that he would march on this city, thus putting the Prussian Army between two fires. In fact he arrived at Leignitz at five a.m., two leagues from the field of battle and returned as soon as he heard of the issue of the combat. The fault he committed was that though at the head of very considerable forces, he had isolated his lieutenant and left no communications with him by means of an intermediate corps, so that he could act in concert, and be kept acquainted with what was happening.

CIV.

On the 20th May, 1800, the French army, after having crossed all the obstacles suffered by the St. Bernard, was stopped by that of the Fort of Bard, effectually closing a defile leading down into the plains of Piedmont. Lannes had made a desperate attempt to carry the fort by assault, but had been repulsed with heavy loss. Bonaparte climbed the lofty rock called Albaredo, being a precipice on the side of one of the mountains forming the pass. With his eagle glances the First Consul perceived the possibility of seizing the town ; it was the work of a moment. He gave orders. One regiment mastered the town, only separated from the town by a torrent. He had the road covered with mattresses and manure, and the guns, carried in strops, passed over at night in the greatest silence, several hundreds of yards within pistol shot of the batteries of the fort. The infantry and cavalry passed by one by one the path over the mountain climbed by the First Consul, and where a horse had never passed before.

CV.

When circumstances oblige you to make a flank march, the enemy must be thrown off the scent. In the campaign of 1796, in Italy, the French occupied Fortona in the first days of May. This forced the Austrian General to retire beyond the Po to cover Milan, and to defend the passage of the Po at Valenza, where he supposed the

French to be crossing. Consequently he placed the troops on the left bank of the Cagna at the camp of Valeggio. Napoléon, seizing the advantage given him by the enemy's false position, took measures to turn their right. He assembled for the purpose a picked division at Fortona, left it very early on the 6th May, and for 18 miles of a forced march turned his flanks to the enemy and marched on Placentia, which he surprised and effected the passage on the morning of the 7th and beat the enemy.

CVI.

There is no more discipline when the soldier begins to pillage, and if he has thereby enriched himself, he soon becomes a bad soldier; he will not want to fight.

Napoléon has said "Pillage is not a French habit; the heart of a soldier is not bad; the first moment of frenzy over he returns to himself. It would be impossible for French troops to pillage for 24 hours; many would employ the last moments to repair the ill they have done in the first. In their messes they afterwards reproach one another for excesses committed, and visit with reprobation and contempt those among them whose acts have been too odious. Never will they have to reproach themselves with having behaved so barbarously as the English at Badajoz and St. Sebastian during the Peninsular war to the inhabitants of those two villages, their allies."

CVII.

At the battle of Millesimo, 14th April, 1796, the Austrian General, Provera, displayed but little talent, which indeed was the real reason which induced Napoléon to praise him in order to gain him credit with the Aulic Council; he succeeded. Provera was re-employed and he allowed himself to be taken a second time, 16th

January, 1797, at the battle of La Favorite through having acted contrary to principles and scattered his army by his march on Mantua to raise its siege.

CVIII.

It is an important rule of policy and morality to treat prisoners of war kindly.

The French alone have treated them with generosity and liberality; thus the Austrians, Prussians, and Russians would willingly remain in France, quit it with pain, and return to it with pleasure.

The lot of the French prisoners in England was very different. They were condemned to the frightful punishment of the hulks, which might well enrich the hell of the ancients if their imaginations could have conceived it. Heaped on one another in unhealthy places, too narrow to contain them, inhaling twice every 24 hours, at low water, the poisonous exhalations. Such was the punishment they suffered for 11 years. Some French Anglophobes go the length of adding: Does it not make one's blood boil to look at that hideous picture of barbarism of which the English oligarchy was alone capable, and which it has carried to its highest point by committing on Napoléon the longest and most horribly consummated murder ever undergone by a living creature in times ancient or modern?

CIX.

This is so true that in the golden ages of the glory of Greeks, Romans, and Spaniards, their armies were patient, disciplined, indefatigable, and never discouraged. The Swedes, under Gustavus and Charles XII., the Russian under Souwarow, were active, intelligent, and energetic.

CX.

Never have the talents of Napoléon been so clearly displayed as in campaign of 1809. The battles of Abensberg, Tendshed, and Eckmuhl were his finest, boldest, and most scientific manœuvre. No epoch has offered such fine examples, such useful lessons, so complete a course of the art of war and the moral theory of military passion. This marvellous campaign of five days, of which each is marked by some trait of genius, by brilliant positions, by a new triumph, may be advantageously studied in the memoirs of General Pelet.

Napoléon, by conforming to the rules of art, has made of war a science of all the great captains; he has conducted the largest armies, fought and conquered the largest of nations; who, like Cæsar and Alexander, has waged war on a mighty battlefield and among many peoples.

Let every officer who would have a perfect knowledge of war meditate well over the campaigns in Italy, above all, in France, his most scientific one perhaps, in which after two years of varying success awakening once on the soil of his country and redoubling his strength, genius, and boldness, he hurries with his brave men, whom his might had brought forth in large numbers, against all the armies of Europe, beats them one after another, and after fabulous exploits was only stopped by treachery. He will be convinced that this great mind never strayed from true principles of war.

CXI.

The best line of defence for a French army against Austrian armies issuing from the Tyrol and Friuli is the Adige; it covers all the valleys of the Po; it intercepts the Mincio, Lower Italy; it isolates the strong place of Mantua.

CXII.

It is for having disregarded this principle that Marshal de Villars failed in the aim of the war of 1733. He was at the head of 50,000 men, in the camp of Vigevano, having no army to face, he could march where he desired. He confined himself to watching on the Oglio, and riding along the Pô. Having thus lost the occasion he did not get it back again until three months after Mercy arrived before Tarruglio with an army. Marshal de Coigny, though at the head of a very superior army during the whole campaign of 1734, and victorious at two pitched battles, those of Parma and Guastalla, gained nothing from all these advantages; he manœuvred in turn on either bank of the Pô. If these generals had known the topography of Italy well, on the very month of September de Villars would have taken position on the Adige, thus intercepting the whole of Italy; and de Coigny would have taken advantage of his victories and reached the spot at once.*

---

* In any great European conflict, Italy is likely to play an important part. Italy remains—apart the mutual rivalry and jealousy of politicians without earnest conviction—a land of deep interest to all countries. Out of every ten travellers, by the way, about Italy, four are English, three German, two Italian, and one Frenchman. From a military point of view, the following War Scheme, supposed to have been prepared for Military operations, may prove of use; it is the outcome of Meetings that took place on the bank of the Lake of Como, between Italian, Austrian and German Generals and Field Officers. Certain Members of the Swiss Federal Council are said to have been present at the Meetings.

1st. It was decided that the whole Italian Army should be placed under the supreme command of the German Staff in case of hostilities. The King of Italy to stay at Rome with the Royal Family.

2nd. Italian troops to be divided into four Army Corps, the bases of operations to be Alessandria, Milan, and Rome for the first three; Naples and Reggio (Calabria) for the fourth.

3rd. The first Corps to be commanded by General Ricotti; General Pelloux —a short while back *décoré* by the French Government on the occasion of the International Shooting Competition held at Rome—to command the Corps which will operate between Pinerola, Col di Tenda and Ventimiglia, with Nice as his objective point. General Ricotti's single care—his marotte—is this invasion of France through the St. Bernard. Napoléon did it : why not a Ricotti ? As to General Pelloux, whose base of operations is the Altenga, he will attempt a crossing of the frontier wherever he can get through, between Ventimiglia and Tenda.

4th. Meantime, another Army, commanded by General Planell, is to invade Switzerland through the upper Ticino, and to endeavour to force his way over the Simplon—Napoléon's fine Military Road—and St. Gothard Passes. A portion of this Army is supposed to have crossed the Austrian Tyrol in order to get down to the Coire (Chur) Valley by the Arlberg Branch of the Alps. After, of course, favourable operations, it would march thence on to either Zurich in order to join a German Army on the Vosges ; or along the Dissentis and Goschenen Valley in order to join the Italians at Brigue on the Rhône, thence to go on to Lausanne and Pontarlier together.

A pleasant and picturesque "Excursion" to be tried on ! were it not for the difficulties to be faced. Unfortunately for the Italians, the Swiss have been building up forts on their own side of the mountains, too ; the Gothard, Coire and St. Maurice (St. Moritz). Again, will Austria—a faithful ally though she be—allow an Italian Army to march across the Trient District after the Italian Agitation that took place on the "dissolution " or breaking up of the *Pro Patria* League by the Austrian Government ? I don't think it likely. Austria is well aware that the Italians would refuse to " quit " their old quarters, if once allowed to revisit its striking and beautiful scenery.

5th. The Third Army is to "cover" the Capital (Rome) and to watch the coast line from Ancona to Castellamare (Castlemari) and from Leghorn to Gaeta. This Army will have to fight the Radicals and Revolutionists and to protect the Vatican. And so as to be able to protect the Pope's seat they will make their " ingress " into his Palace quietly, the Pope having removed to his country place at Castel Gandolfo, near Albano, beforehand, *tout naturellement*. European Powers, fortunately, are not unaware that Italian Radicals are more of a match against Italian Troops *than the Pope*.

In the event of hostilities with the Foreigners, Italian Revolutionists would prove a matter for grave anxiety all over Italy from Milan to Bologna, from Bologna to Rome and from Rome to Naples. It would be " all up " with the King and Royal Family in Italy, should the smallest reverse take place during the war. For the Radicals and Revolutionists would revolt throughout Italy in a body, if they had not done so already on war being declared. The Third Army will indeed have a tough job to get through—looking after the King, Royal Family and Pope all at the same time.

It is as well that the Head-Quarters Staff and the Body of Military Officers throughout Italy are intensely devoted to their King and Royal Family. Every member of the Italian *famille militaire* is ready to act as Pallavicini de Prisla did at Aspromonte when he ordered his men to shoot down Garibaldi who was wounded at the *heel!* The same fate is reserved, without the slightest doubt, to General Riccio Garibaldi—the coming hero of the Italian ever-restless Irredentists—by Italian Officers who will kill the first man who dare rebel against the King of Italy or try to transgress the laws that protect the interests of Italian unity. It is only natural. Marchese Carlo Alfieri di Sostegno—whose death is a sad blank in Italian Politics—is a man whose life should be given as an example to the younger generation of Italian Aristocracy to follow; a devoted Liberal friend of the House of Savoy and none the less a good Catholic. The Marchese was a "gentleman," an aristocrat *au bout des ongles*, and a right Christian. He is the founder of the Scuola di Scienze Social at Florence, for the training of the sons of the upper classes for Political life. As to Ricci Garibaldi, he is his father's own son, and all is going as merry as a gong with him for the present. We shall hear about him and his proposed Federal Republic for Italy under the Presidency of the Pope, before long. He must keep a sharp look-out! Harm hatch! Harm catch!

It is only natural, too, for us to add the following statistical account about the population in France from a Military point of view on account of Conscription in case of War, in England.

In the year 1801 Great Britain was a long way behind France, who then had nearly twice our population; but in the present year, 1899, we have succeeded in getting an appreciable lead over France to the extent of about two millions of population. In 1801 France's population was over twenty-seven millions. In 1801 our population was under sixteen millions. In 1851 France's population was under thirty-six millions. In 1851 our population was over twenty-seven millions. In 1899 France's population is thirty-eight and a half millions. In 1899 our population was forty and a half millions. Thus in 1801 we were (nearly) twelve millions fewer than the French; in 1851 we had reduced the French lead to under nine millions, and in the present year we lead France on the score of population by almost exactly two millions of persons. We outran France in population for the first time in the history of the world in 1893 or 1894.

This is a falling off in the French population which should be seriously considered by the thoughtful ones in France for a while, along with her National Debt of heavy THIRTY milliards of francs, as set forth in her Budget Bill for 1900! It is a patent factor of weakness against the very national existence of France when compared with her neighbours.

At any rate, as to Italy, it is as well to note the opinions of the following two Military experts worthy of our attention, and, finally, to remember what they

say. "The Army of Italy commands respect," writes General Baron Haymerlé, after a long residence at the Court of the Quirinal as an Australian Military Attaché; while another Military Authority across the Western Alps—"L'Armée française en 1879" p. 438—remarks:—
"*L'armée italienne, dont l'organisation si bien étudiée est à présent si remarquablement avancée, sera, je crois pouvoir l'annoncer, incommode aux adversaires qu'elle rencontrera dans les guerres à venir.*" (L. E. H.)

PART III.

THOUGHTS RELATIVE TO THE ART OF WAR.

1st.—The mind of a good general should resemble in clearness the glass of a telescope, which has been under the grinding stone, and presents pictures to the eye.

2nd.—Generals make their name by victories or great deaths.

3rd.—Nothing inspires more courage, and clears one's ideas more than to know the position of the foe.

4th.—War is like government, a business of tact.

5th.—The tactics of war should be changed every ten years, to retain its superiority.

6th.—The fate of a battle is the result of an instant of thought; the armies approach with various combination, join battle, fight for a certain time, the decisive moment arrives, one moral spark gives the word and the smallest reserve carries it out.

7th.—In all battles, a moment always arrives when the bravest soldiers, after having made the greatest efforts, feel disposed to fly. This terror arises from a want of confidence in their courage; it needs but a trivial occasion, or pretext to restore this confidence; the great thing is to arouse it.

8th.—There is a moment in all fights, when the most petty manœuvre decides the day, and gives success. It is the drop of water which makes the overflow.

9th.—There are several ways of occupying a given position, with the same army; the soldier's eye, the experience and the talent of the chief, will make the decision; that is his chief office.

10th.—It is necessary in war to profit by every occasion, for fortune is a woman; * if you let her slip to-day, do not expect to find her to-morrow.

11th.—Not to be surprised at not obtaining victory, think only of defeat.

12th.—It is an axiom, people being credulous as they are, when an enemy obtains reinforcements, to receive some also, so that the belief of equality may be maintained.

13th.—Success in war depends on a glance and a right moment.

Napoléon said in his Memoirs, that his decisive victory of Austerlitz would have been lost if he had attacked six hours later.

14th.—Being inured to fighting, having superiority in tactics, and coolness in command, alone make victorious.

15th.—Kind and gentle behaviour befit the victor alone, but are a dishonour to the conquered, whose qualities should be reserve and pride.

16th.—It is with States as with a ship at sea, or an army, coolness, moderation, wisdom, reason, are needed in the conception of order, commands, or laws; energy and vigour in their execution.

17th.—In war as in policy, every evil, even when partly done, is only excusable when absolutely necessary; anything more than that is a crime.

---
* *Fortune* a goddess is to fools alone.—(DRYDEN.)

18th.—In war as in policy, the lost moment never returns.

19th.—Military fanaticism is alone good for anything; a man needs some of it to risk his life.

20th.—The first qualities of a soldier are fortitude and discipline; courage but the second.

21st.—A soldier follows the fortunes or misfortunes of his general, his honour, and religion.

22nd.—A soldier should know how to overcome dejection and melancholy. It is as true a courage to meet with constancy the pain of the soul, as to meet without flinching the fire of a battery. To abandon oneself to grief without resisting it, is to go and kill in order to get rid of it.

23rd.—The vigorous rules of military discipline are necessary to guarantee the army from defeat, slaughter, and especially dishonour. It must look on dishonour as worse than death. A nation can recover men, but not honour.

24th.—Military crimes should be judged with promptitude and severity.

25th.—The true reward of armies is the good opinion of their fellow citizens.

26th.—There is nothing great of which a Frenchman is not capable.* The love of glory is for him a sixth sense.

27th.—In the siege, as on the field, it is the cannon which plays the principal part.

28th.—Nothing is more destructive than the charge of artillery on a crowd. We can avoid one or two bullets, but it is almost impossible to escape 18 or 20.

---

* Justice apparently is absent at present under the French Republic. (L. E. H.)

29th.—Not to be afraid to die, is itself a terror to the enemy's ranks.

30th.—Armies are not enough to save a nation, while a nation defended by the people is invincible.

31st.—Revolutions are a fine time for soldiers of mind and courage.

32nd.—It is always in times of trouble, and especially after a victory of the people, that there are born the elements of a national force, which becomes the army called on to save a country.

33rd.—When once the torches of a civil war are lit, military chiefs are not the makers of victory; it is the crowd that governs.

34th.—In civil war it is not given to every man to know what to do; it needs something more than military prudence; it needs wisdom and the knowledge of men.

35th.—In party warfare he who is vanquished once is disheartened for a long time; so it is especially in civil war that fortune is necessary.*

---

* Count Bismarck told Mr. Malet (Sir E. Malet), Secretary of the English Embassy at Paris, in 1890, at Meaux, that the Prussians meant to have Metz and Strasburg, and should remain in France until they were obtained. The Prussians did not intend to dismantle, but to make them stronger than they then were. "The French," he said, "will hate us with an undying hatred, and we must take care to render this hate powerless." Frenchmen have been talking loudly and long enough of their intention to re-conquer them. Until now the difficulty of the task has prevented—and will prevent for a while—the attempt. However strong a man's resolution may be, it costs him something to carry it out now and then. We may determine not to gather any cherries, and keep our hands sturdily in our pockets, but we can't prevent our mouths from watering. Animal antagonism is the word for Franco-German racial hatred; and this hatred will never die. So it is with the latent dislike between the calm, tenacious-of-purpose, practical Englishman and the eager, impulsive, quick-witted Irishman. I dare not say as much of the shrewd, canny Scot, or the unflinching, determined, and energetic Welchman. Racial antagonism and dislike are *latent* between Saxon and Celt; they are open between Frenchmen and Germans; that's all. This disposition exists, at any rate, in the public life of the day, and in official positions within our very Army, Navy, and Churches in England.

And again, the Germans are not a war-loving race, but they are a brave race,

36th.—In certain circumstances military qualities are of avail only; civil virtues exert perpetual influence on the public happiness.

37th.—Laurels are no longer so when covered with the blood of citizens.

38th.—Military, public, or administrative business, demands strong powers of thought and analysis, and the ability of concentrating mind on a point without fatigue.

39th.—Conquered peoples do not become subjects of the victor except by a mixture of policy and severity, and by their amalgamation with the army.

40th.—The ground is the general's board, and its choice will testify to his skill or ignorance.

41st.—Every party chief should know how to use enthusiasm; there is no faction without its fanatics. The greatest general, with soldiers without enthusiasm, is but a fool.

42nd.—One is rarely supported by one's inferiors except when they know you are inflexible.

---

who will not embroil the Continent in war for an *idée*, for the power of shifting glory, or for even the interests of their Imperial dynasty. In the present condition of some depressing influences in European public thought, it is not out of place to remind French Republicans that the Germany of 1899 is not the Germany of Jena and Austerlitz. Doubtless William II.—a Christian Prince, a strong and able Ruler—is not underrated by the *élite* of France as a foe close on the French track "afloat" and "on shore"; nor as a "right" Royalist Politician, who has none in him of the "tender and intelligent" sympathy for the depressing and anti-European Republican politics of the Pope, and of English Catholics towards France (a country born and bred the first Catholic and Royalist Land in Europe). Much as I sympathise with France, I am glad, on the other hand, for the sake of Europe, that she has had her military prestige well tried lately, which has been the cause of most of the wars in Europe during the last two hundred years. And, for the sake of entire France at home, I shall be glad to see Paris lose its political prestige and reduced to the political helplessness of London or Berlin *versus* Country; for the rule of Paris, politically, has ever been, and is, a curse and a blight to France as a vigorous and progressive body. (L. E. H.)

43rd.—A state will never get capable officers but by a careful education, and by protecting the sciences applicable to military or naval war, to the arts, to agriculture, to the preservation of the human beings.

44th.—A battle is a dramatic action, which has its beginning, middle, and end. The order of battle taken by the two armies, their first advances to meet one another, are the prologue; and the counter-movements of the attacked army forms the knot which renders new dispositions necessary, and brings about the crisis, whence arises the result or catastrophe.

45th.—True courage and warlike talent are never amazed at anything, and will not falter before any kind of hardship.

46th.—The general who does great deeds is he who possesses at once civil qualities, a good eye, calculation, mind, administrative knowledge, eloquence, not of a lawyer, but suitable to the leader of armies, and lastly, the knowledge of men.

47th.—The important secret of war is to make oneself master of the communications.

48th.—A general in war should know but three things; to march 10 leagues a day, fight, and canton afterwards.*

---

* What, then, about the following words uttered by Napoléon III. to the King of Prussia before Sedan, September 1st, 1870:—" Sire, my Brother—Not having been able to die in the midst of my troops, it only remains for me to resign my sword into the hands of your Majesty.—I am, your Majesty's good Brother, NAPOLEON." Since Pavia (24th February, 1525) no French monarch had been taken in battle or siege. At Pavia, King Francis I. surrendered only *after fighting with heroic valour and killing* SEVEN *men with his own hand*. "Sedan" is the darkest spot in the chequered military history of France; no modern nation in Europe ever received such a crushing blow. Thus fell ignominiously the Empire, and ended the reign of Napoléon III., which had kept the world *sur les épines* and France amused for twenty too-long years. (L. E. H.)

49th.—In war every movement should aim at gaining a good position.

50th.—Military genius is a gift from Heaven; but the most essential quality of a general is firmness of character, and a resolve to conquer at any price.

51st.—In mountain warfare an army should never attack, but wait to be attacked; *vice versa* on the plains.*

52nd.—Battles should never be engaged unless you can calculate on 70 favourable chances. Battle even should not be delivered unless there is nothing else to hope for, since by its nature, the fate of a battle is always doubtful; but once it is determined on, there is nothing but to conquer or to die.

53rd.—It is on the care given to the battalions in depôt that the quality and durability of an army depend.

54th.—Every army on its first trial bears, with difficulty, the tests to which it is exposed, and if it has, besides, a long march to make, it grows less in proportion to the distance.

55th.—With a raw army it is possible to carry a formidable position, but not to carry out a plan or design.

56th.—In war prudence advises to prize the foe at its just worth, and more than he deserves if you do not know his strength.

57th.—The qualities suited to offensive warfare are: activity, audacity, and a good eye, also intelligence and resolution.

58th.—Soldiers who are resolved to die, may always save their honour, and often their liberty and life.

---

* *Quærendum est?* (L. E. H.)

59th.—A retreating army should have a little start in order to sleep and eat. It should not have the enemy too near; for to suffer an attack when on the march, and with back turned, is a most dangerous way of receiving battle. The wisest thing then is to choose its own ground and wait battle.

60th.—No river, or any line whatever, can be defended without having offensive points, for when we have made arrangements only for defence, we run risk without obtaining security. But one may combine defence with an offensive move; we make the enemy run more risk; but also greater losses can be inflicted on the body which has been attacked.

61st.—In war nothing is got but by calculation; anything not thought out in all its details effects no result.

62nd.—The whole art of war consists in a well ordered and prudent defensive, and in a bold and rapid offensive.*

63rd.—All is opinion in war, opinion of the enemy, opinion of one's troops.

64th.—After the loss of a battle, the difference between conqueror and conquered is but a petty one: it is the moral influence which is everything, since two or three columns are sufficient then to produce a great effect.

65th.—In war one needs healthy and precise ideas.†

66th.—The art of war has principles which it is never permitted to violate.

67th.—In war we take our course before the enemy; we have night always in which to get ready.

---

* General Sir Redvers Buller adds another duty common enough, yet most serious. The gallant Officer says: "It is of great importance in war that every Commander should remember his REAL OBJECTIVE." (L. E. H.)

† "Les illusions sont plus funestes que les mauvaises intentions, parce que celles-ci ont une limite, tandis que les illusions n'en ont pas." (L. E. H.)

68th.—In war all is mental, and the mind and opinion make up more than the half of reality.

69th.—A great general has made it a point to make the enemy think his troops very numerous, and impress upon his own men that the enemy were very inferior.

70th.—To change a line of operation is work for a master mind; to lose it is so disastrous that it makes the general who does so guilty of a crime. Thus, it is necessary to guard it, to be in communication with his depôt, where he can get rid of the prisoners he has made, of his sick and wounded; find provisions and a rallying point.

71st.—According to the laws of war, every general who loses his line of communication deserves to be shot. I understand by a line of communication that in which are the hospitals, succour for the sick, ammunition, provisions, where an army re-organize, recruit, and regain in a few days' rest its moral lost by some unforeseen accident.

72nd.—We do not call it losing one's line of operation, when it is harassed by partisans or insurgent peasants, for these could not face the van or rear.

PART IV.

SOCIAL AND POLITICAL THOUGHTS.

INTRODUCTORY REMARKS.

NAPOLEON'S SHARE IN THE PROGRESSIVENESS OF
EUROPE.

The following lines refer to the non-military side of the life of Napoléon. On 22nd June, 1815, Napoléon surrendered the Royal Crown which his ambition and vanity had duped him into usurping. Not happy enough was he with his prosperous and astounding career as a soldier. Success had turned his head, and he had lost sight, on 30th April, 1804, of the grand principle laid down for man's safety: *The soul of man is a garden where, as he sows, so he shall reap. If ye would gather roses, do not sow rotten seeds.* WATERLOO and SEDAN speak to you, reader, and to me for themselves as a ludicrous and terrible vindication, at the hands of God, of Napoléon's answer to Cámbacères on that day: *J'èspère que la France ne se repentira jamais des honneurs dont elle environnera ma famille.*

The KING OF FRANCE was guillotined on the 21st of January, 1793. But the monarchy could not be deposed and abolished, and the Royal Family of France had as its new head a Prince conscientious and constantly attentive to the exalted duties of his station—Louis XVIII. (*Comte de Provence*, brother to Louis XVI.) The Royal Crown of France was INALIENABLE, and IS STILL; it could not be made over to even the most lucky plebeian of the XIXth century— Napoléon Bonaparte. *Humanity is d——d rascality*, however. Heaven forbid I may be thought over censorious by so saying. *Probatum est.*

On 2nd November, 1802, flushed with victory and desirous of solidifying his authority as First Consul for life, Napoléon had come forward and made most tempting overtures of a "substantial" nature, which he hoped would prove acceptable to and indemnify Louis XVIII. SUBSTANCE! SHEKELS! What a powerful influence in giving a strange direction to some people's conscience! The mesmerizing Golden Calf ever was a big item in the political inventory of French Republicans and Imperialists—Siamese twins they are. But the "substance"— the shekels—acted not as an attraction but as a scarecrow to the honourable King of France, who rejected Bonaparte's fatuous bribe and advances worthily, and wrote: "*M. Bonaparte établirait mes droits, s'ils pouvaient être litigieux, par la démarche qu'il fait en ce moment.*" As upstarts do under plebeian régimes of "democratic competition," Consul Bonaparte sought beyond all doubt, of course, and in the last resort, to "buy" the King; he it was who was "sold."

It has been an extremely interesting inquiry to the historian, however saddening, to trace the mischievous effects of Napoléon having exceeded the powers and the rights of his legitimate ambition on the course of French Politics; as much concerning the national peace and happiness of France as concerning her international influence. *Probatum est.* Following the logic of facts, I say fearlessly that I regret the decline of Royal Absolutism and Aristocratic supremacy at any rate in France, all things considered. Of the two evils offered for my choice: either an Absolute King, assisted by a supreme Nobility and Gentry, with security associated with peace and law; or a plebeian Empire or a Republic, under which a Sergeant-Major is told insidiously by "democratic" Chiefs that he may bloom into a Field Marshal in the Queen's army through war: I prefer Absolutism and I would cast in my lot with the King. In any case, I love little the political rash haste of Frenchmen, their plots and conspiracies, their chicanery and intrigue, and their native violence under any political " Ism." Dr. Shadwell, Hon. Fellow of Oriel College, was not wrong to sound the foghorn against them in his Latin speech on 22nd June, 1899—Commemoration Day at Oxford—when introducing Lord Kitchener and Mr. Cecil Rhodes for the reception of their D.C.L., *honoris causâ* at the Encænia. The experience of recent years of "democratic competition," politically, militarily, and socially in this country against old-fashioned freedom, supports my opinion about France. Happily, English taste and habits are manifestly not in favour of " democratic " administrators, even with jack-boots and spurs; Englishmen will stand up against degrading tutelage whatsoever. I read the following notice in the *Morning Post* of July 14, 1899 (Column 6, p. 5): "*To-day being the date of the French National Fête, the French Ambassador will receive the French Colony at Albert Gate House, Albert Gate, from 4 to 6 o'clock.*" I noticed *en-passant* the day after that the First Secretary—not the Ambassador—it was, who "received." My point, however, is that the "14 Juillet," is now a household word in French mouths just like the "15 août" was under the Empire before 1870. Has it occurred to some of my readers to ask

Napoléon's War Maxims. 141

—reasonably enough—the meaning of this French NA-
TIONAL Fête to be presided over and so religiously kept
in London by the Official Representatives of French
Republicanism at the Court of English Royalty? The
French Ambassador, by "receiving" his Republican
fellows on 14th July, means them to recollect that the " 14
Juillet," is the Red Letter Day of French Republicans.
It is the commemoration of the day on which, in 1789, the
Paris mob rose to the height of its madness, and, by the
common reckoning, began the French Revolution. This
they did by storming the Bastille, dragging the Governor
and the officers in charge to the Place de Grève,* cutting off their heads and hands, and carrying the latter
on pikes through the streets.† The bloody character
of a French mob only too prominently showed itself
there as it did at the Roubaix lion-bull-fight on July
14th, 1899; and as it did at the sacking and firing of St.
Joseph's Church, in Rue St. Maur and St. Nicholas in
Rue St. Martin at Paris on Sunday, August 20th,
1899. If my historic explanation seems not straight
and true enough to my readers, they will help me by
inquiring at Albert Gate House further. For romantic
interest and intrinsic importance, too, I, in my turn,
invite the Representatives of French Republicanism in
London to read Napoléon's *Thoughts* 63rd, 207th, and
276th in this Book. I pass on.

It comes to this : Napoléon fell—forty years old only
—leaving France brought back to her former boundaries
as before his appearance. Yet his victorious armies
had over-run Europe, and marched through every
European capital leaping with joy: Lisbon, Madrid,

---
* To-day Place de l' Hôtel de Ville.

† The Commemoration is celebrated now usually by a Military Review
under orders of the Republican Government and by general " boozing " and
dancing at the expense of local Municipalities. (L. E. H.)

Rome, Naples, Turin, Milan, Munich, Berlin, Warsaw and Moscow—yea, Alexandria and Cairo. His material work disappeared after him soon as brief as a soap-bubble; but he outlived himself as the actual representative of the French Revolution, whose principles he spread about the world without a pang of remorse. He had started on his political and social course of usurpation, saying: *Je suis la Révolution!* He kept his word. In England not a few persons became Jacobinical in their views, and the Government found it necessary repeatedly to suspend the Habeas Corpus Act. In the first place, Napoléon was welcomed gratefully by Frenchmen as the fortunate man before all Frenchmen, who saved French Society by quelling insurrection. Just as Prince Henry d'Orléans did welcome a few weeks ago the Galliffet-cùm-Millerand Cabinet—the queerest craft afloat — simply because anything, everything is good-enough, that the family may grow wiser and happier in France, where for the nonce, scarcely anyone dares to utter his real sentiments —as base and unnatural a national life and habits as those which sway the minds and customs of ring-nosed and tattooed-faced heathens. General de Galliffet is an officer and a gentleman; and not the "tiger in human form" as represented by Mr. C. Healey. He is a man of civil as well of military courage, who neither equivocates nor prevaricates. His joining the Republican "crew" simply meant his love for his native land, for his beloved Army; but self-love? No. I admire and respect General de Galliffet for his indeed genuine patriotism. But there is no real fight in the Republican braggarts, political quacks and lucre-hunters whom he has to "muzzle." Their own skins are dearer to them than even the persecution of the supporters of Kings and Queens, justly called Royalists. But in the next place Republicans tripped up Napoléon because he was the main-stay of Revolutionary principles. To these did not Napoléon owe his deplorable accession to the throne of Royal France? And this is why the Napoleonic Legend has remained the record of a once famous truth among most famed men, but the record, too, of a man who did half his task only; or rather who went through it all, if you like, but doing the right at one time, doing the wrong at another, leaving both France and Frenchmen finally victims to grievous and melancholy Utopias, and to deadly feuds of which the effects have brought on the disorganisation and decay of France. Waterloo, the Revolution of 1830, the Revolutionary explosion of 1848, with its series of fearful concussions, Sedan, and the collisions of 1870-71, have left the France of our own times poorer in leading men and in secure institutions than at any other period of her history. *Gradatim*, decade by decade, a misgoverned nation gets nearer and nearer to her fall—not instantaneously; meantime the strong States are becoming stronger. The French to-day have but one choice: *Le Roi ou un Cercueil.— Erudimini, qui judicatis terram!*

Napoléon's enterprising and organising genius, his strength of body and will, his love of glory and the immense power which the Republican party put into his hands, made Napoléon the most gigantic figure of modern times. That which would have made the destiny of an ordinary person remarkable, counts for little in his. Springing from obscurity and rising to supreme power, from an artillery officer, having become the great leader of Nations, he dared to imagine a Universal Monarchy, and for a moment realised it.

After having obtained the Empire by his victories, he wished to subdue Europe by means of France, and England by means of Europe. In order to do this he established a military system against the Continent, and the blockade against Great Britain. This design succeeded for several years, and from Lisbon to Moscow he subjected States to his will, and imposed upon them vast sequestrations of property—*Anglicè* "Territorial acquisitions."

But he failed to persevere in the conciliatory mission given him on the 18th day of Brumaire (9th November — Lord Mayor's Day ! — 1799), to pacify France. Bonaparte was not born with the nature of Diocletian who, after a reign of twenty years, wearied of the purple, and sighed for his native Dalmatian Hills, then subject to the sway of the Roman Empire. Diocletian's name reminds me that his abdication was one of the earliest in the history of the world ; and when he was urged once more to take up the sceptre of Imperial rule, he replied : "If I could show you the cabbages I have planted with my own hands at Salona, you would no longer urge me to relinquish the enjoyment of happiness for the pursuit of power." By exercising, for his personal advancement, the powers he had received ; by attacking the liberty of the people by despotic institutions—"*Je jure*," he swore unsheathing his sword on that day, "*de percer le sein de mon frère*,* *si jamais il porte atteinte à la liberté* "—and the independence of States by war, Napoléon injured both the interests, the opinions and feelings of the human race all round. He aroused universal enmity ; and even the French nation began to withdraw its allegiance from him. After having been victorious for so long ; after having

---

* *Lucien Bonaparte*, President of the Council of Five Hundred.

hoisted his standards on all the capitals of Europe, and on the magic charm-inspiring Pyramids; after having, for ten successive years, increased his power and gained a kingdom and a crown with each battle, a single reverse re-united the world against him, and he succumbed in proving how impossible despotism is in our day. *Probatum est.*—"*It is only by judging of results that you will arrive at a just and confident judgment.*"—(Marquis of Salisbury.)

Nevertheless, setting aside the disastrous results of his system, Napoléon gave a prodigious impulse to the latent forces of the Continent. His armies carried with them the customs, ideas, and the more advanced civilization of France. Modern societies have been roused and re-organised on their old foundations. Nations got mingled by frequent communications, bridges got thrown over rivers separating neighbouring countries, great highways were opened, yea, *cut* through the Alps and Pyrenees—and thus territories got drawn nearer together. In fact, Napoléon did for the material welfare of States what the French Revolution claims to have done for the minds of men.

The Blockade completed the impetus of Conquest; it perfected Continental industries in order to supply the place of those of England, and it replaced Colonial commerce by the produce of Manufactures. It is thus that by arousing nations, Napoléon has contributed to their civilization or progressiveness. His despotism with regard to France, however, was as mean an abuse of power as insolent a breach of oath. In his speech against Napoléon on 25th May, 1815, Henry Grattan said:—
"Gentlemen speak of the Bourbon family. I have already said we should not force the Bourbons upon France; but we owe it to departed (I would rather say

interrupted) greatness to observe that the House of Bourbon was not tyrannical. Under her, everything, except the administration of the country animadversions; every subject was open to discussion—Philosophical, Ecclesiastical, and Political—so that Learning, Arts and Science, made progress. *Even England consented to borrow not a little from the temperate meridians of that Government; her Court stood controlled by opinion, limited by principles of honour, and softened by the influence of manners; and on the whole there was an amenity in the conditions of France which rendered the French an amiable, an enlightened, a gallant and an accomplished Race.* Over this gallant race you see imposed an Oriental Despotism. Their present Court (Bonaparte's Court) has got the idiom of the East as well as her constitution; a fantastic and barbaric expression; an unreality which leaves in the shade the modesty of truth, and states nothing as it is, and everything as it is not. The attitude is affected, the taste is corrupted, and the intellect perverted. Do you wish to confirm this Military tyranny in the heart of Europe?" At the same time Napoléon's conquering spirit made him the regenerator, and in a fair way the tinker of an almost motionless Europe in which several Nations, drowsy until his coming, will henceforth live by means of the life he breathed into them: Prussia and England in the front rank.

But in these things Napoléon merely obeyed his nature. Born of war, war was his delight and pleasure; power his ruling ambition. He almost conquered the world; and circumstances—I call these "The Unseen Hand"—put it at his feet in order that it might be able to draw fresh life from him.—"*If ye would gather roses, do not sow rotten seeds.*"

LUCIEN HENRY.

BOOK I.*

1st.—Respect will be paid in the day of their humiliation to those who have respected themselves in the day of their power.

2nd.—Ten persons who speak make more noise than 10,000 who are silent; this is the secret of the barkers of the tribune.

3rd.—There should be no half responsibility in the administration, it will only cause peculation and the non-performance of the laws.

4th.—In the world it is not faith that serves, it is mistrust.

5th.—In business there should be neither prejudice nor passion except for the public good.

6th.—Ambition to sway other minds is one of the strongest of passions.

7th.—Ambition is to man what air is to nature; take the one from his moral and the other from his physical principles, and he will cease to move.

8th.—Strong minds repel pleasure, as a sailor avoids rocks.

9th.—When we know that we are suffering from a moral disease we must take care of our soul, as we would of an arm or leg.

10th.—The power of thought appears to be an attribute of the will; the greater the perfection of reason, the greater is that of the soul, and the greater the responsibility for its actions.

---

* Napoléon's military work is ever interesting to a soldier and his advice valuable. But when we come to his non-military work, we may have to ask the reader for his endurance to hold out a little longer. I am afraid the unsentimental and "irreverent" Englishman, after reading through one of Napoléon's non-military thoughts or two, will feel inclined to pitch them away from Folkestone to Boulogne and ejaculate B-o-s-h ! *Sint ut sunt, aut non sint.* (L. E. H.)

11th.—An enemy is more anxious to hurt, than a friend to help.

12th.—Would you count your friends, fall into misfortune.

13th.—Love is a business to the idle man, a destruction to the warrior, and a rock to a Sovereign.

14th.—The only victory in love is flight.

15th.—It is indecision and anarchy in the contriver which cause indecision and anarchy as the results.

16th.—Anarchy is the stepping stone to absolute power.

17th.—The yoke of the English is relished by no nation. All suffer with impatience the dominations of these islanders.

18th.—Englishmen despise all other peoples and especially the French. That nation barters as freely master-pieces of art, as the liberty and prosperity of other peoples.

19th.—It is by money that we must secure lovers of money.

20th.—A State without an aristocracy, is a vessel without a rudder, a balloon in the air.

21st.—A democracy may be furious, but it has a heart, it can be moved; an aristocracy is always cold and it never pardons.

22nd.—We may stop ourselves when going up, never when coming down.

23rd.—The Sciences which do honour to human mind, the Arts which beautify life, and transmit great deeds to posterity, ought to be specially honoured by Free Governments.

24th.—Audacity may undertake everything, but not do it.

25th.—It is a sound principle to make frequent changes in Officers and garrisons; the good of the State demands that there should be no situations immovable.

26th.—Man may perhaps calculate a few, often deceitful, probabilities, but the future is in the hands of God.

27th.—When it is sought to make a policy law, the lawyers always oppose of it.

28th.—Anything not founded on bases physically and mathematically exact, should be banned by the reason.

29th.—If you want a thing done well, do it yourself.

30th.—True social happiness lies in the regularity and harmony of one's enjoyments, and suitability to each other.

31st.—Those who seek for happiness in pomp and dissipation resemble those people who prefer the waxlights to the light of the sun.

32nd.—Good sense makes men capable; self-love is the wind which swells the sails, and brings their vessels into harbour.

33rd.—Gallantry is inborn, not instilled.

34th.—A great reputation is a great noise, the more there is of it, the further does it swell. Land, Monuments, Nations, all fall, but the noise remains, and will reach to other generations.

35th.—It is only with prudence, wisdom, and much dexterity, that we can attain great ends and surmount all obstacles, otherwise no success.

36th.—Everything in life is a subject of calculation; we must hold the balance between the good and the bad.

37th.—It is always vile and dishonouring to calumniate the unfortunate.

38th.—In administration as in war, character is essential to success.

39th.—A constitution is of use when acted upon only ; the Chief of the State should not be a partisan.

40th.—Civilization does everything for the mind and favours it entirely at the expense of the body.

41st.—In all centuries and States, circumstances have called for extraordinary laws.

42nd.—The code of the safety of nations is not always that of private men.

43rd.—Nothing so good in the world as a good heart.

44th.—Commerce unites men and makes them, therefore is it fatal to despotic power.

45th.—Our conduct may be shaped on reason and calculation.

46th.—Genuine victories and the sole conquest yielding no remorse are those over ignorance.

47th.—True conquest, ones leaving no regret behind, are those made over ignorance.

48th.—A constitution supported by an aristocracy resembles a ship. One without is a balloon lost in the air. A ship can be directed because there are two forces to balance one another; the rudder forms a point of support, but the balloon is a toy of one single force, the point of support is wanting, the wind carries it away, and direction is impossible.

49th.—It is a great mistake at Court not to push oneself forward.

50th.—That unshakeable courage which, in spite of most sudden catastrophes, leaves the mind, judgment and power of decision as free as before, is indeed rare.

51st.—Practised prostitutes despise the idol they seem to adore, and are always ready to break it.

52nd.—If in a nation, crimes or delicts increase, it is a proof that misery is increasing, that the society is ill governed.

53rd.—The contagion of crime is like that of the plague; criminals being associated together, corrupt one another; they are more hardened than ever, when after the expiry of their sentence, they emerge once more into society.

54th.—All transaction with crime, becomes a crime on the part of a Crown.

55th.—Ceremonies are to religion what external garments are to men in power.

56th.—Cynical manners are the ruin of the body politic.

57th.—Nothing is more difficult, and therefore more precious, than to be able to decide.

58th.—Declamations pass away, but nations remain.

59th.—The great proof of madness is the disproportion of one's designs to one's means.

60th.—An enlightened nation is not to be governed by half measures; there must be force, consistency, and unity in all the public acts.

61st.—A man may lose his popularity for a slight fault. As for a "*coup d'état*," when he knows the way to rule he will not risk his credit but on good security.

62nd.—Despotism, though transferred from the hands of the Ruler to those of the ruled, is none less despotism.

63rd.—Republican despotism is more fertile in acts of tyranny, because everyone has a hand in it.

64th.—Drawing and the exact sciences gives correctness to the mind. Drawing teaches one to see, and mathematics to think.

65th.—The first of virtues is devotion to one's country.

66th.—Under a Master in political life, to talk of the rights of the people, is a criminal blasphemy.

67th.—With the old edicts of Chilperic and Pharamond, there is no one who can say that he is exempt from being legally hanged.

68th.—The Church should be a part of the State, but not the State of the Church.

69th.—It is in times of difficulty that great nations, like great men, display the whole energy of their character and become an object of admiration to posterity.

70th.—Prison, blood, death, create enthusiasts and martyrs, and bring forth courage and desperate resolution.

71st.—In all our designs we must assign two-thirds to reason, one-third to chance. Increase the first fraction, you will be over cautious; increase the second, you will be rash.

72nd.—When honours are thrown away lavishly many will get them who are unworthy of them, and more will be in the shade. They will not go and seek for the Knighthood on the field of battle, when they can get it in an Office.

73rd.—Political balance of war is a dream.

74th.—The human mind has made three important conquests—the jury, equality of taxation, and liberty of conscience.

75th.—When the wit sparkles and the passions speak, reason and judgment go to sleep.

76th.—He who cares not for the esteem of his fellow citizens is unworthy of it.

77th.—Public esteem is the reward for good people.

78th.—Constitutional States have no springs, the action of the government is too trammelled; this it is which makes them inferior in their struggles with powerful and absolute neighbours. A dictatorship might help them, but the ram is at the door of the Capitol before they are ready.

79th.—There are events of such a nature that they are above the human organization.

Napoléon's War Maxims.

80th.—The true wisdom of nations is experience.

81st.—Every faction is an aggregate of dupes and duped.

82nd.—A man is weak because of want of exertive power or of self-confidence, when he is so for both these reasons; if he is but a private man, he will never be much; if he is a king he will be lost.

83rd.—Weakness in the supreme power is the most frightful calamity for peoples.

84th.—We must recognize human weaknesses, and bend to rather than combat them.

85th.—Nothing is more imperious than weakness supported by force.

86th.—Fanaticism is always the product of persecution.*

87th.—In mind under the influence of fanaticism there is no outlet by which reason can enter.

88th.—Of 100 royal favourites, 95 are not worth hanging.

89th.—It is a woman's lot to soften our crosses.

90th.—A beautiful woman delights the eyes, a good one the head; the former is a jewel, the latter is a heart treasure.

91st.—In finance, the best way to obtain credits, is not to make use of it; taxation strengthens it, borrowing destroys it.

92nd.—Finances founded on good agricultural prospects will never be destroyed.

93rd.—Flattery is a mark of a government weak in mind or power of ruling, just as the seditious call despotism a strong will.

94th.—Flatterers are legion, and not one of them can flatter in a noble and decent way.

---

* Not always. Ex.: Mohammedanism or Islamism with its 200,000,000 followers; also Buddhism and Brahminish with their 672,000,000 votaries.

95th.—Fashion condemns us to many follies; the greatest is to make oneself its slave.

96th.—The follies of another will never make us wise.

97th.—Force is always force, enthusiasm always the same, but persuasion remains and engraves itself on the heart.

98th.—The surest lever to power is a military force sanctioned by law, and at the command of talent. Such was the conscription. It is enough to consider this force, contradictions will be effaced, power strengthened. What matters, after all, the reason of sophistry, when there is a strong ruler? Those who obey are compelled to confine themselves to the line of the order law lays down for them. At length they grow accustomed to the yoke, draw the sword, and the factions return to their native dust.

99th.—Machiavel talks in vain, fortresses are not worth the favour of a people.

100th.—We must follow fortune in its caprices, and correct it as we can.

101st.—The French will be worth their full price when they substitute principles for turbulence, pride for vanity, and love of institutions for love of places.

102nd.—With all our expansion and mobility, why are French people always complaining?

103rd.—Our ridiculous national fault is to have no greater enemies to our success and glory than ourselves.

104th.—Babbling is a national characteristic of the French since the days of the Gauls.*

---

* Frenchmen will censure and damn me for my following words, no doubt. But I say that as a nation, whatever may be their courtesy in all their relations and civility in their wildest moments, French people are not reliable. The Roman race is not. They may poison your name, if not your porridge, or run a slit through a mutual contract, if not through you, doing it, as Isaac

105th.—The Frenchman, by nature, is active, restless, and a babbler.

106th.—The sentiment of national honour is never more than dosing with Frenchmen; but a spark is needed to light it.

107th.—The French love greatness even when it is but a show.*

108th.—French people have two equally powerful passions which appear opposed, and which, however, arise from the same temperament: love of equality and love of honours. A government cannot satisfy these two wants except by strict justice. The law and the action of the government should be equal to all; honours and rewards should fall on men who appear in the eyes of all to deserve them the most.

109th.—The French nation is easiest to govern when it is smoothed down the right way. Nothing equals its prompt and easy comprehension; it finds out at once

---

Walton did with the worm, "as though they loved" you. Diplomats and City men can tell. Again, Frenchmen are endowed with more physical than civic strength; they prefer to shut their eyes to what is *désagréable* than to face and to grapple with it *à l'anglaise*. They call "sublime heroism" what an Englishman calls, "right funk." (L. E. H.)

* Frenchmen fight for the power of GLORY; Germans for BUSINESS; Englishmen for ENGLAND.

"The German Army may have many excellent qualities, but chivalry is not among them. War with them is a business. Like the elephant, which can crush a tree or pick up a needle, they conquer a province and pick a pocket. As soon as a German is quartered in a room, he sends for a box and some straw; carefully and methodically packs up the clock on the mantlepiece and all the stray ornaments which he can lay his hands on; and then, with a tear glistening in his eye for his absent family, directs them either to his mother, his wife, or his lady-love. Pianos they are very fond of. When they see one they first sit down and play a few sentimental ditties, then they go away, requisition a cart, and minstrel and instrument disappear together. They are a singular mixture of bravery and meanness." — (*Diary of the Besieged Resident in Paris*, p. 374.) Ben Battes and his New Englanders in New Orleans might have profitably taken lessons from these all-devouring locusts (L. E H.)

those who are working for or against it. We must appeal to its senses, otherwise it is gnawed by a restless spirit, boils over, and is carried away.

110th.—France is a country where chiefs have little influence; to depend upon them is to build upon sand. Great things cannot be done in France without the support of the masses; besides, a government should seek its support from the right quarters. There are moral laws as imperative as physical ones.

111th.—Coolness is the grand quality for a commander.

112th.—Talent will not guarantee one from the miseries of life.

113th.—Nature should bestow its gift of talent so that it may be of use to the dunce; but often talent is out of place, and like a seed which is stifled in its growth and produces nothing.

114th.—Bold men should not be sought for from those who have anything to lose.

115th.—Some people keep straight because they have not had the opportunity to go wrong.

116th.—There are men who are over-obliging, as some are always insulting. We must be neither one or the other; for in either case the reason of their good deeds will be criticised.

117th.—The caprices and passions of the governing body, being once enchained, the interest of the people march without hindrance in their natural path.

118th.—Men are more easily governed through their vices than through their virtues.

119th.—In matters of government partners are needed, otherwise the play will not be done through.

120th.—Governments with balanced force are of no good but in times of peace.

121st.—At bottom the name and form of the government is but of little moment provided that justice is rendered to all the citizens, that they are equal before the law, and the State is well governed.

122nd.—Every government should not view men but as a whole.

123rd.—It is the conjunction of interests which constitutes the true strength of a government, for to combat them is to expose oneself to certain death.

124th.—A government which is composed of natives, and maintains itself without the aid of the foreigner, is a National Government.

125th.—Property, civil war, love of country, are the ties of every government.

126th.—A ruler, at bottom, must be a soldier; a horse is not ruled without boots and spurs.

127th.—To rule one must govern with head and not with heart.

128th.—It is difficult to rule, if we wish to do so conscientiously.

129th.—Nineteen-twentieths of those who rule do not believe in moral inferences; but they deem it their interest that people should be persuaded that they make a good use of their power. Thereby alone they are called honourable.

130th.—That they should be truly free, the governed should be wise men, and the rulers gods.

131st.—The greater a man becomes, the less will should he display; the more dependent is he on events and circumstances.

132nd.—There is nothing beautiful but what is great; extent and immensity may cause defects to be pardoned.

133rd.—It is never useful to make oneself hated and arouse hatred.

134th.—Chance is the only lawful monarch of the universe.

135th.—Men must be led by their present bridles, and not by their future ones.

136th.—Men sunk in degradation are never conspirators.

137th.—In the eyes of founders of great empires, men are not men, but instruments.

138th.—The great man is he who is by nature unimpressionable ; praise or blame will affect him but little ; it is his conscience he listens to.

139th.—To become a good man, one must have faithful friends, or outright enemies.

140th.—Men fashion themselves after circumstances.

141st.—How many great men are children more than once a day.

142nd.—A man never distinguishes himself in life, but by controlling his natural character, or by creating a new one, and being able to modify it according to circumstances.

143rd.—One does a bad deed who is an honest man at bottom, another commits a wicked act, without being a wicked man. Man never indeed acts by the natural bent of his character, but by a secret passion of the incident hidden in the innermost recesses of his heart.

144th.—The man, who is really a man, never has an enduring hatred ; his anger and ill-will never last more than the moment.

145th.—A man in authority should never look at persons, but at things, their weight and consequences.

146th.—Man is no safer at the edge of a rock, than under the canopies of a palace. He is a man everywhere.

147th.—Man is a difficult being to know; in order not to be deceived, we must judge him by his actions, and especially those of a moment and which last but a moment.*

148th.—Men have their virtues and their vices, they are heroes to-day and cowards to-morrow; they are not all good or all bad altogether; but they possess in them, and make use of all that is good or bad here below; that is the fundamental principle. Nature, education, and accidents are its applications. Beyond that, it is all spurious systems, all wrong more or less in this world.

149th.—All men are equal before God: wisdom, talent, and virtues alone make differences between them.

150th.—Men must be led by an iron hand in a velvet glove.

151st.—Miserable men that we are! Weakness and error, that is our motto. We can do nothing against the nature of things, our own remaining power is to observe.

152nd.—No man can rise high enough to get out of reach of the blows of fate.

153rd.—Men are ciphers and acquire value by their position.

154th.—Men, like pictures, need to be shown in a good light.

155th.—A disheartened man is undecided, because all courses seem to him bad in the affairs of life; the worst evil is indecision.

156th.—Man is sheep-like, he follows the first passer-by.

157th.—Do not believe a man's words unless his actions prove them.

158th.—In no society can man pass as good and just, if he knows not whence he comes and whither he is going.

---

* "*Il y a de grands et de petits pays; les hommes ont partout la même taille.*"—An admittedly precious remark from a Diplomatist who has been taught more than one wholesome lesson, no doubt, His Excellency the Portuguese Minister to the Court of St. James, DON LUIZ DE SOVERAL. (L. F. H.)

159th.—Men as a rule make more use of their memory than of their judgment.

160th.—The heart of a statesman should be in his head.*

161st.—The surest support of man is God.

162nd.—Opportunities are often less wanting to a man than perseverance and will.

163rd.—Nothing which degrades a man can be useful.

164th.—Men are pleased to be wonder-struck.

165th.—The man who allows himself to be governed by his wife, is neither himself nor his wife; he is nothing.

166th.—There is nothing worse than a good man in political crisis, when his mind is fascinated by false ideas.

167th.—Nations and parties as a whole are more fruitful than they think to the sentiment of honour, to glory, and national independence.

168th.—Those who seek for honour resemble a man in love, possession diminishes its value.

169th.—All the details of life should be submitted to its rule; to be able to overcome one's ill-temper.

170th.—There is nothing purely ideal which has not some atom of the positive, and false seed by careful management produces good fruit.

171st.—He who can carry in his mind most images, is one gifted highly with powers of imagination.

---

* Bonaparte's Empire is resulting evidence of the man's belief of that maxim, although the Capitulation of his nephew at Sedan not only scorched it, but killed. The pride and vanity of every Frenchman were after 1870 the strongest evidence that Napoléon spoke from experience as regards French people at any rate. An ever-restless race ruled by pot-house politicians to-day, and helpless all round. Evidence of this I can see plainly in the subserviency of the French Republicans to Germany, who cares not a bean for the Republic, as contrasting with their foolish and obstinate Anglophobia. (L. E. H.)

172nd.—Immorality is indubitably the most disastrous failing for a ruler, in that he makes it a fashion, for to please him, people will give it a good name, it strengthens all other vices, it saps all virtue, it is the curse of a nation. Public morality, on the contrary, is the natural complement of all laws; it is in itself a whole code.

BOOK II.

173rd.—Since the discovery of printing, knowledge has been called to power, and power has been used to make it a slave.

174th.—Indecision in a prince is to government what paralysis is to the motion of the members.

175th.—True industry is not to execute by the use of all the means given and known; it shows talent and genius to do in spite of one's faculties, and to find thereby nothing impossible or next to it.

176th.—A healthy mind braves misfortune, and displays noble courage in resisting it.

177th.—Men are powerless to secure the future; institutions alone fix the destinies of people.

178th.—The best institutions become vicious when morality ceases to be their basis, and when their officers are but led by egotism, pride, and insolence.

179th.—Their interest which turns men from pole to pole is a language which they learnt without its grammar.

180th.—The most astonishing of inventions are not those of which the human mind may be proud; it is to a mechanical instinct and to chance, that we owe the majority of our discoveries, and never to philosophy.

181st.—The just man is the image of God on earth.

182nd.—Without justice there are but parties, oppressions, and victims.

183rd.—In matters of government, justice means force as well as virtue.

184th.—Justice depends on the public order. The judges are on the top-most rung of the social ladder, they could not be surrounded by too much honour and consideration.

185th.—Legislation is a buckler which Government should bear wherever the public prosperity is attacked.

186th.—Certain things are called legitimate because they are old.

187th.—Political liberty is indeed a fable drawn up and imagined to quiet the governed.

188th.—The law should be clear, precise, and uniform; to interpret it is to corrupt it.

189th.—What is called natural law is but that of interest and reason.

190th.—Laws in theory a model of clearness, become often chaos when applied.

191st.—All the evils and plagues which may affect men come from London.

192nd.—To discharge the duties of a Magistrate needs the most profound respect, and the most absolute devotion to the great interests of the State.

193rd.—The power of magistrates is weakened when they live on familiar terms with the advocates of the prisoners they are to judge.

194th.—Everyone is not master in his own house.

195th.—A man can suffer from having eaten too much; never of having eaten too little.

196th.—When the community, as a whole, is corrupted, laws are almost useless without a despotism.

197th.—The men who have changed the universe have never done so by changing the chiefs, but by stirring the masses.

198th.—Vengeance visited on the bad is a reparation to virtue.

199th.—The poor man commands respect; the beggar must always excite anger.

200th.—It would be a curious book which contained no lies.

201st.—It is wrong to grant to a name the prerogatives which are due only to merit.

202nd.—Merit is pardoned, not intrigue.

203rd.—The strength of ministers of religion consists in the exhortations of the pulpit and in confession.

204th.—Ministers of religion should never meddle in civil matters; they should always bear the mark of their character, which, according to the spirit of the gospel, ought to be one of peace, toleration, and conciliation.

205th.—Moderation gives dignity to governments as well as to nations. It is always the companion of the strength and durability of social institutions.

206th.—Wisdom and moderation are of all countries and ages; but they are as absolutely necessary to little states as to commercial towns.

207th.—Republics cannot be made out of old monarchies.

208th.—The world is a great comedy, where you find 100,000 Tartufes for one Molière.

209th.—Old replastered monarchies last only till the people feel its own strength; such edifices perish always from their foundations.

210th.—In morality alone is true nobility, if not there it is nowhere.

211th.—Public morality is founded on justice, which, far from excluding energy, has proved to be the grand result of it.

212th.—The laws of morality are conjectured, like those of ontology. It is therefore the characteristic of a higher mind.

213th.—Life is strewn with so many snares, and may be the source of so many ills, that death is not the greatest of them.

214th.—Death is a dreamless sleep.

215th.—Among the persons who seek for death there are few who find it when it would be a boon to them.

216th.—The noblest death is that of a soldier dying on the field of honour, if the death of a judge, perishing in defence of his Sovereign, throne, and laws, were not more glorious still.

217th.—Calculation is good when there is a choice of means, and it is boldness which will carry the day otherwise.

218th.—Of all the liberal arts music has the most influence over the passions. The legislator should, therefore, encourage it. The chorus of a song produces a more affecting effect than a moral treatise.

219th.—To divide the interest of a nation is to injure them all. It is impossible to divide things naturally indivisible.

220th.—When it comes to pass that a certain class have gained the power of suing for lucrative posts, a nation has lost true freedom, nobility, and dignity of character.

221st.—Poor Nations! Despite your knowledge of wisdom you are still in submission to the caprices of fashion, just like ordinary private people.

222nd.—They who think that nations are flocks who belong by Divine right to certain families, are opposed to the spirit, both of the age and of the gospel.

223rd.—The law of necessity subdues the inclination, will, and reason.

224th.—Neutrality consists in having the same weights and measures for each.*

225th.—Oligarchies never change their opinions, because their interests are always the same.†

---

* *Quærendum est.* For example: China (1899) has refused to allow horses purchased for the United States to be shipped to the Philippines on the ground that they are contraband of war. In America this is regarded as being near to a recognition of the rebel Aguinaldo's belligerency against the Americans. Is China's perversity a case of neutrality dutifully kept from an International point of view? I call it a case of dutiful perversity. (L. E. H.)

† The Commonwealth, or Republic of the crafty and despotic Regicide Oliver Cromwell was, *cela va sans dire*, a caprice of Democracy, fickle and considered dangerous by Foreign Courts. "The Czar of Russia chased the English Envoy from his Court. The Ambassador of France was withdrawn on the proclamation of the Republic." (J. R. Green.) " Because he (Oliver Cromwell) was a *usurper*, he became of necessity a despot." (Southey.)

Let it not go unremembered that in the Ages of Christian Faith, Kingship and Royalty were considered as an inviolable shrine. Regicide or King-killing and murderous attacks on Crowned Heads and Heads of State, have increased in frequency since the Reformation and the Renaissance. Kingkilling has got looked upon as no longer a guilt so abominable from the time when Brutus and Scevola got received and honoured as heroes. Charles I., Mary Stuart, Henry III. and Henry IV. of France, Louis XVI. and his Royal Family were the first victims to fall under this pagan reaction. Now-a-days murderous attacks on Royalty and Heads of State have grown so general that Democracy—"the backbone of England"!—rather look upon such murders as a trifling felony.

And at the risk of being described as not found guiltless of vanity, cynicism, or selfishness by certain co-religionists, I have thought a fact worth while "booking" which I read in *The Morning Post* (August 4th, 1899), about the Cromwell Memorial proposed to be erected at Huntingdon. It will remain a query of wonder in English History from the Catholic point of view why the Marquis of Ripon has recently been honouring Cromwell's memory by subscribing a sum of "two figures" towards erecting a statue to the English "King-killer." It may seem uncourtly of me to enlarge on this pecuniary subscription given by the Marquis of Ripon, unimportant *en apparence*, rather than on the appeal made for the one now open towards putting up a statue to Simon de Montfort. But Lord Ripon is to me not only one of Her Majesty's former Chief Officers of State, also an ex-Viceroy of India and the ex-Grand Master of the Freemasons of England. The noble Lord is a "convert" Member of the Roman Catholic Communion and the President of the important and virtuous Brotherhood of St. Vincent de Paul's Patronages, established in Eng-

226th.—The Church ointment, though it attaches us to the Kingdom of Heaven, does not deliver us from the infirmities of the world, its villainy and abominations.

227th.—Public opinion is a power invisible, mysterious, and irresistible.

228th.—All becomes easy when we follow the current of opinion ; it is the ruler of the world.

---

land in 1844, for visiting the poor in their own homes, the care of homeless and destitute Boys and Foundlings, and other charitable works. Lord Ripon ranks as "Grand-Master" of this Catholic Society, and as "Lord Protector" of his new, poorer, and untutored co-religionists. A Parliamentary Candidate in search of political vote and influence at any future time might have been found not thick-ribbed enough to refuse his "two figures"; and then even, a loyal Catholic would accept no such barter. But Lord Ripon is past the age of Political Vote-asking and power-seeking ; and the noble Lord's fealty to the English "King-killer" is to me—a Catholic—an object lesson with a voice potential in the petty conflicts and agitations of a Country, as regards the future. I dare believe that even his "honorary patronage" would have been refused by the late President, George Biount, to the Cromwellian Memorial. "The born fighters are always true to their salt." I am a teacher. In these days of religious mutiny and confusion we hear a great deal about the educational value of "Creed": but the English "King-killer" was dead against the "Romans"—was he not ?—whom he would have treated as the pariahs and outcasts of English Society. Indeed several priests were condemned to death for exercising the functions of their priestly office ; and one actually suffered the extreme penalty—while self-called religious independency or religious liberalism of the Cromwellian "tolerance" brought on the appearance of the numerous sectaries, who thought themselves free and of sufficient ability to build up a religious system for themselves, the most singular being the Quakers, the Muggletonians, and the Millenarians or Fifth-Monarchy men (these gave Cromwell no little trouble). I have, my Lord, studied religions in England during the Commonwealth ; and as an old friend and supporter of the Brotherhood of St. Vincent de Paul, of which I am a member, I reject your Lordship's system, not suitable to a Catholic mind, of associating Catholicism and Cromwellianism. The faults of the children of the Church are no disgrace to the Church, any more than the faults of God's creatures are a disgrace to their Creator. But none the less Lord Ripon's prominent position—which alone secured him the Presidency of St. Vincent de Paul's grand Brotherhood—gives his political example of Cromwell worship an equally prominent position. I will have my students believe me when I say that I call it consistent for any Catholic—Prince, Peer, People —to subscribe to a "Manning Memorial." Cardinal Manning was Christian and Catholic, England's worthiest worker in the XIXth century, and a noble rival to St. Vincent de Paul as a *pater patriæ* and a tutelary Saint

229th.—Nothing is more fickle and vague than public opinion, and yet, whimsical as it is, it is trustworthy, reasonable, and just more often than one thinks.

230th.—Public opinion ought to be the thermometer a Sovereign should frequently consult.

231st.—Among those who like not oppression, are many who like to oppress.

---

of Humanity. Cromwell is not one of those persons who have had a share in making England great. Simon de Montfort, at any rate, is the founder of the great English House of Commons (the legitimate pride of Englishmen and the envied jealousy by Foreigners). Cromwell was a diabolical, useless, and dangerous worker in England, Scotland and Ireland. And therefore the "King-killer" should sleep undisturbed and unremembered, except as a warning to younger Englishmen and to Catholics against "Republican—Monarchists" and popular leaders whose motto political is "King-killing no Murder." I said "Republican—Monarchists." Such amphibia there live in these days again whose titled names are printed within the clasps of the English "Snob's Bible."

St. Vincent de Paul says:—"*Il vaudrait mieux être jeté pieds et mains liés parmi les charbons ardents, que de faire une action pour plaire aux hommes.*" Then at the risk of seeming to hold too complete an independence of action, I further my Royalist Creed by resting my plea on Lord Ripon's saintly protector above. And I further my opinion finally that the upper and more cultivated classes should not "give in" to the Republic in France by resting my plea, as the test of truth, on the maxim of another Catholic personage, St. Vincent de Lerins, "*Quod ubique, quod semper, quod ab omnibus.*" Now, the Nations of Western and Eastern Europe, and the more hopeful breed of humanity across the Atlantic, Pacific and Indian Oceans—at Hawaii even!—are *Royalist*, the bulk of them. *Ergo* "nappy" the Pope, Peer, or Plebeian feels who counsels rallying to a Republic or to an Empire the bulk of whose workers are "Republican-Monarchists," vulgar blusterers, and bad men in France. The learned Mr. Thomas Terrell, Q.C., who fought North Paddington in the Liberal interest at the 1892 election, says, in the introduction of his pleasing and accurate "Holiday Notes" addressed from Rennes to the *Kensington News* of August 25th, 1899:—"The Republic as it at present exists is closely associated with Freemasonry." Let Englishmen bear in mind that French Freemasons are sworn Atheists religiously, King-baiters politically, and the movers and makers of the Divorce Court across the Channel. Three qualifications, little honourable and most unsavoury, with French men and women as a nation, believe me. The France veracious, honourable and pure, is not Republican, as Sir Ellis Ashmead Bartlett says rightly. The Throne and the Catholic Church have been the two-fold mainstay of France in the past. I believe that their attraction and power are recovering; and the sooner the better, for the repute and the rank of France as a Nation. *Encore*

168   *Napoléon's War Maxims.*

232nd.—The great orators who charm assemblies by the brilliancy of their words are, in general, but second-statesmen. It is no use to fight them with words; theirs will always be more sonorous; their eloquence must be met with clear logical reasoning, their power lies in vagueness; bring them back to the reality of facts, to the practical, and they will be crushed.

233rd.—Without order the administration will be in a chaos, no finances, no public credit, and with the fortunes of the State the fortunes of individuals will also crumble away.

---

un peu de temps with her present Republic; then France—still fair, good, and lovable after all—would become a *Maison fermée*, disliked and to be avoided by every man and woman of education and culture. Albert-Gate House would have to shift out of the neighbourly vicinity of Buckingham Palace; and French Diplomats on its Republican Establishment would get blackballed at the St. James's under the International Public Health Act while suffering from a dangerous infectious disorder not to be spread in any street, public place, shop, inn, or public conveyance in London and outside the Metropolis!

The following three books will teach Englishmen much about the present state of Freemasonry and Catholicism in France, as far as they interest any man not hypnotised in matters of conscience under the magnetism of the three snares of Satan.

(1) LE VATICAN.—*(Les Papes, la Civilisation et le Gouvernment de l'Eglise—La Papauté à travers l'Histoire—l'Administration pontificale—les Papes et les Arts—la Bibliothèque vaticane)* with an introduction by H. E. Cardinal Bourret and a conclusion by M. le Vicomte E. Melchior de Vogüé, of the French Academy.

(2) *La France Chrétienne dans l'Histoire*, with an introduction by His Em. Cardinal Langénieux, of Reims.

(3) *L'Irréligion contemporaine et la Défense Catholique*, by the Rev. P. Fontaine, S.J.

Mask himself as he may, even the unfaithful Roman Catholic will avow to you that there is an irreconcilable enmity between the Catholic Church and Freemasonry. Not because English Freemasons are servants, friends, flatterers of any anti-Christian spirit or system; but simply because a *French* Freemason, as a secret society man, is understood within the Catholic Church in France to mean the malicious spirit of Anti-Christ. And from its malice the vile reptile has not changed; the Jewish and Infidel war to the knife going on under the Republic, convulsing Catholic France and horrifying Christian Englishmen, saves me the necessity of saying more.

A Republican Catholic in France is either an utopian dupe, or a lick-spittle and unreliable *âme damnée*—a "base deception"! (L. E. H.)

234th.—The sphere of materialism is extremely limited, truth must be sought for in morality, if one would sound the depths of policy and war.

235th.—The social order of a nation depends on the choice of the men who are to keep it up.

236th.—Order marches with weighty and measured strides, disorder is always in a hurry.

237th.—Paradise is a centre whither the souls of all men are proceeding ; each sect in its particular road.

238th.—To be deprived of one's natal chamber, of the garden where one's infant feet have pattered, is to have lost one's country.

239th.—Forgiveness will raise a man above one who insults him.

240th.—Love of country is the first virtue of the civilized man.

241st.—One's country cannot shift about ; it is immovable and is wholly on the sacred soil which has given us birth, and where the bones of our fathers rest.

242nd.—The surest way to remain poor is to be an honest man.

243rd.—A fool is only troublesome, a pedant insupportable.

244th.—People who are masters in their own house are never tyrants ; that is why a king who knows not contradiction is a good king.

245th.—Perversity is always individual, hardly ever collective.

246th.—The rights of the chief are only those of the people. The right of the people is to submit itself to the laws.

247th.—A people which abandons itself to excess, is unworthy of freedom ; a free people is one which respects persons and property.

248th.—The people's judgment is sound when it is not led away by agitators.

249th.—There is nothing but patience for people when it has fallen under the yoke of a great slavery, their instinct will warn them of the circumstances which may deliver them.

250th.—A people have no strength but in nationality.

251st.—When people cease to complain, they cease to think.

252nd.—People recover from every reverse, except that of consenting to their dishonour.

253rd.—It is only those who would deceive a people and rule them for their own profit, who would keep them in ignorance.

254th.—The best philosophy is to gain happiness by the practice of right.

255th.—Love of place is the greatest blow to the morality of a nation.

256th.—When a man has an absolute want of a situation, he is already "sold" in advance.

257th.—The requisites of a good police officer are a want of passion and prejudice, patience in hearing and judging, never deciding without having given reason time to recover.

258th.—Absolute power has no need of a lie; it is silent. Responsible Governments obliged to speak acts and lies shamelessly.

259th.—All becomes easy to power, when it wishes to direct in the ways of justice, honour and joy around.

260th.—From lawyers, it is not easy to get simplicity.

261st.—Bad priests insinuate their fraud and lying everywhere.

Napoléon's War Maxims.

262nd.—A good prince should have the deportment of Cæsar, the manners of Julian, and the virtues of Marcus Aureleus.

263rd.—A Prince is despised, when he is weak and irresolute; it is much worse when he is governed by an incompetent or inconsiderate minister.

264th.—Princes who have confessors are a contradiction to Royalty.

265th.—It is by wounding the self love of princes, that influence is gained over their deliberations.

266th.—Vulgar Sovereigns are never despots with impunity.

267th.—The ancients conciliated men of various conditions; we separate them most distinctly.*

---

* This is an excellent maxim, from which Englishmen may be sensible perforce of the political wisdom of England's recognition of the Italian Unity. English Catholics are divided into two camps as regards Italy: the "White" Catholics, who back up the Quirinal, and the "Black" Catholics, who support the Vatican. Nations, like individuals, are not partial to advice; and it is not for us to judge whether a Catholic will be "lost" who shows himself unwilling to kiss the Pope's *mule*. Protestant countries merely notice the jealousy between the Vatican and the Quirinal. And as to England's policy towards Italy, it may be summed up in a few words: Catholics in England feel that the friendship betweeen Protestant England and United Italy, the regard and affection which King Humbert enjoys in England, and the fact that the Anglican Church does not acknowledge the control of the Pope, inevitably efface both the Pope and his representatives in England in the calculations of English politicians and of English Society. But England is also aware that Italians themselves are against Papal rule. A telling fact: the plebiscite which took place on October 22nd, 1870, in the Papal States, gave FOR the Unification of Italy under one King out of 167,548 voters, 133,681 against 1,507. The rest did not vote. *Vox populi, Vox Dei?* English opinion (though Protestant as a Creed) is that the interests of Italy are identical with those of England in the Mediterranean Sea; Englishmen feel a warm admiration for what Italy has done since her unification. They respect her political constitution, and they sympathise with her legitimate aspirations. Englishmen are for a Royal Constitution and freedom of thought for Italy as for England, and they consider patriotism the first of virtues. They admire the organization of the Roman Catholic Church, and they respect the Roman Catholic religion. They do so, however, as they do Judaism in the City Money-Markets and Mahometanism by the waters of the Ganges. They

268th.—Reason, logic, a definite result first, should be the guide and aim in all sublimary matters.

269th.—Without the Bible, we are marching in darkness. The Catholic religion is the only one which gives man safe knowledge as to his beginning and last end.*

270th.—Let dogmatic controversies never do harm to the sentiments which religion inspires and commands.

271st.—If a Government needs for its stability a dominant Church, it will reject a dominating Church.

272nd.—To ask how far religion is necessary for the State, is to ask when to tap a sufferer from dropsy.

---

do so because these three creeds are a potent lever for patriotic purposes in skilled hands But Englishmen don't care twopence for "priestly twaddle," and have no sympathy with the Vatican aims on Temporal Power. In the opinion of Englishmen such matters are questions not of sentiment in the hands of sophistical or deceitful workers, but of political expediency. No nation, they think, can get on without a religion ; no State can be governed without a firm hand at the helm. But whether the religion is Budhism or Roman Catholicism matters very little to an Englishman, so long as the mass of the people BELIEVE IN IT AND ACT UP TO IT. So, too, the Head of the State or Church should do : *Noblesse oblige*. (L. E. H.)

* This is piety covering conspicuous hypocrisy on Napoléon's side, and cunning simulation which "brings grist to the mill," as evidenced by the most shocking falsity of his following reply. On his return from Russia to Paris, Napoléon was anxious to turn French minds from his unhappy failure in the North, and desirous to get them to believe that France's prestige and power were in no danger. To what, then, do you think this *Catholic-born* and *Catholic-crowned* Ruler, plausible enough and bold when his vanity and hopes were on the luck-way, attributed France's trials and her sorrows through his own mishaps in Russia ? To the unmeaning and trifling word IDEOLOGY ! And he defined this ill-adapted expression and this sort of mental state as a "Tenebrious Metaphysics." I call that "Hallucination" on his part. In these modern days this disease is termed "hysterics" by Specialists in both Medical and Philosophical Schools, who say that it betrays a general breaking up of the system, because it has its roots within the mind in certain patients, and in the perversion of their senses in others. The surgical operation of both the surgeon and philosopher at the same time is absolutely needed for the recovery of strength by the willing patient As a foreign writer and a way-worn traveller about different countries, and with men of education and culture, to my mind the ideal man is not Napoléon as a Civilian ; an Englishman is my ideal man. A comparison will usefully illustrate my meaning. As a foreigner watches the well-dressed cohorts who invade the City of London every morning for their *affaires* of many kinds, he may notice the trustworthy,

273rd.—Religion is the reign of the soul, it is hope, it is the anchor to save us from misfortune, it is the ministry of morality, right principles and good manners.

274th.—Policemen and gaols are not the ways to bring back to the practices of religion.

275th.—It is easier to establish a republic without anarchy than a monarchy without despotism.

276th.—There can be no republic in France; the *bona fide* Republicans are idiots, the others intriguers.*

---

solid, commanding and obvious honesty of the Englishman's character which belong as little to the "Yankee Agents"—his nearest kinsfolk. Why so? Because in Napoléon appearances were not facts. To my mind, as a Frenchman, diametically opposed in blood, creed, and politics, to English public opinion as represented by the London press to-day, I pride myself to publish that my ideal man of all men is the *English gentleman*, whose appearances are facts, and who makes appearances go hand-in-hand with the grave responsibilities of both the citizen and the city man, with the smallest depth of sparkling excitement and special pleading. I have read it: the late Mr. W. H. Smith was looked upon as the type of such ideal Englishman. But my tutor at Cambridge gave me the name of Mr. John Bright, as an Englishman whose type might be a lesson to me, a Frenchman, as valuable as any of the enduring characters, morality, and success of an Englishman in whose appearances were facts, and facts were appearances. And I have found good many ENGLISH " John Bright " since I left the University for the wide world, I feel it right to state. But the history of dejected and exhausted France permits me to assert that Napoléon cut a poor figure as a Civilian ; and as a Catholic Frenchman. (L. E. H.)

* Sir Ellis Ashmead Bartlett's subjoined letter to the *Morning Post* of August 19, 1899, is evidence telling about Napoléon's above remark from an outsider thinking about France. It is the consciousness that he is acting in the spirit of self-sacrifice, as well as his fervid vindication habitually of manifest and undefended rights—whether "above" or "below"—that cause the thrilling cheer ever given the Honorable Member of Parliament for the Sheffield-Ecclesall Division, from the ranks of patriots " unbought." Sir Ellis was recently upraiding, justly and in time, the Press of England for their forced or unforced partisanship and auxiliary corporation in the saddening Rennes Court-Martial Case. And the Hon. Member, in truth, " puts the saddle on the right horse " when he says :—" The curses of France, the attacks on the French people in our Press, are becoming *excessive and irrational.* The Dreyfus affair is bad enough, but it is not fair to involve the whole French people in a common condemnation. The evil and the scandal from which France is suffering are due to two causes. (1)

277th.—In every well regulated household, we ought to expend but the one fourth of one's income for the kitchen, the one fifth for the stables, and the one ninth for the dwelling.

278th.—Jealousy is the characteristic of popular risings; equality of interests commences them, concurrence of passions continues them, and often they end by civil wars between the insurgents themselves.

279th.—Never is there a social revolution without a terror. The best of them destroy everything there and on, but replaces them in the future.

280th.—In a revolution everything is forgotten. The good you have done to-day will be forgotten to-morrow. The face of things once changed, gratitude, friendship, relationship, all ties are broken, and each one seeks his own interest.

281st.—A revolution is one of the greatest curses which can fall on a land. It is the scourge of the generation which effects it; all the advantages it can procure cannot make good the trouble with which it has filled the lives of its authors. It enriches the poor who are not satisfied; it overturns everything. In its first moments it makes its misfortunes for all, the happiness of none.

282nd.—In revolutions there are two kinds of people: those who make them, and those who profit by them.

283rd.—He who prefers riches to glory is a spendthrift who borrows at usury and who ruins himself in interest.

284th.—Riches do not consist in the possession of treasures, but in the use made of them.

The Republican system of government. (2) The unchecked licence of the Press. Until an effective law of Press libel is established and enforced, there can be little hope for France. The second evil also prevails in the great American Republic, and with results almost equally disastrous. These are the real enemies of France—the Republic and an unbridled Press." (L. E. H.)

285th.—The true wealth of a state consists in the number of its inhabitants, in their toil and industry.*

286th.—Riches are not the usual lot of the soldier, and of the Judge who must be indemnified by having consideration and respect. The regard shown them keeps up the point of honour which is the true strength of a nation.

287th.—A king cannot afford to give in before misfortune.

288th.—A king should be above the worst blows of misfortune.

289th.—A king is not a king of nature, but of civilization; he must march at its head, he is never naked, but must ever be clothed.

290th.—It is the weak or wicked king who associates himself with the vulgar passions of his inferiors when he should be repressing them.

291st.—Kings only love people who are of use to them, and only as long as they are so.

292nd.—Kings only show attachment for the benefits they confer, and never for the services rendered to them; and that because in the first case, they love their creatures, and in the second their self-love revolts at the thought of their being the obliged; for it is always placing oneself in an inferior position, to feel obliged to anyone.

293rd.—The overthrow of prejudices has laid bare the source of power; kings and princes cannot help getting crafty.

---

* The Duke de Sully, King Henri IV.'s Financial Minister, was fond of reminding His Majesty of the following wise fact truer than ever to-day: *le labourage et le pastourage, voilà les deux mamelles dont la France est alimentée, les vrayes mines et trésors du Pérou.* Sully is on the right scent here rather than Napoléon. Here, too, we may be allowed to remind our readers of Sully's *Economies Royales* (a sensible book). (L.E.H.)

294th.—The Ribbon of an Order is a stronger bond than chains of gold.

295th.—Ribbons may adorn courtiers but not men.

296th.—If science were taken in hand by power, it would produce great results for the well-being of society.

297th.—Severity prevents more crimes than it represses.

298th.—The fool has one great advantage over the learned man, he ever feels in a state of quiet peace with himself.

299th.—The observations of a fool teach us the degree of simplicity to which we must descend to be understood by all.

300th.—One may be a fool with wit, but not with judgment.

301st.—The Sovereign has but one duty to discharge to the State: to get the law observed.

302nd.—A weak Sovereign is a calamity for his people.

303rd.—The Sovereign is always wrong to speak in anger.

304th.—A Sovereign should only promise what he can perform.

305th.—The honour, glory, and happiness of a Sovereign can never be other than the honour, glory and safety of the people.

306th.—The aim of a Sovereign is not only to reign, but to spread instruction, morality, well-being. All that is false is poor help.

307th.—A Sovereign never avoids war when he likes; but when he is forced to fight, he should hasten and draw the sword himself, and be the first to make a quick invasion, without which all the advantage is on the side of the aggressor.

308th.—Sovereignty cannot travel; it is inseparable from the territory, and remains bound up with the mass of the citizens.

309th.—Sovereignty should always display itself in full vigour; granting petitions, and ever above petty human infirmities.

310th.—It is but one step from the sublime to the ridiculous.

311th.—Success makes the great man.

312th.—Suicide is the act of a gambler who has lost his all; or of a ruined prodigal.

313th.—Suicide is the greatest of crimes. What courage can he have who trembles before a reverse of fortune? True heroism consists in being superior to the evils of life.

314th.—As a matter of system, one ought to reserve to oneself the right of laughing over one's ideas the day after they have occurred.

315th.—A political system cannot go on in which words clash with deeds.*

---

* Manifestly lucky on the fields of battle and frantic with his One Monarchy Scheme for the whole of Europe, Napoléon *se méconnut* and belied this 315th Political Thought of his. All *parvenus* behave not otherwise. Here follows our evidence as to Bonaparte's case.

In 1804, the amiable and pacific Pius VII. had journeyed to Paris at Bonaparte's invitation and crowned him an Emperor. The poor old Pope had thought this a political deed necessary to the security, the interest, and the honour of the Catholic Church. A disgusting farce the Coronation ceremony was on the part of Bonaparte, nick-named the "Prince of superstitions" by his fellow-Republicans, who all had sworn, with him, to *purge* France of Royalty and Aristocracy! Anyhow, Napoléon had written to Pius VII. shortly *after his* coronation a letter which he got published throughout the country, and in which he had said:—"*The Emperor has always thought it useful to the cause of Religion that the Sovereign Pontiff of Rome should be treated with every regard due to him, not only as the head of the Catholic Church, but also as an independent Sovereign.*" (This same opinion he expressed in his memoirs later on, when a prisoner himself, at his last resting place on earth—St. Helena.) Yet he dared and feigned high and mighty to disregard his own

316th.—Rashness succeeds often, still more often fails.

317th.—There is one kind of robber whom the law does not strike at, and who steals what is most precious to men, *i.e.*, time.

318th.—A head without memory is a place without a garrison.

319th.—Is not theology reserved for Heaven? Why here below make God the subject of our discussions?

---

political advice to others by depriving the same Pius VII. of his temporal States (17th May, 1809) and by locating him a prisoner, first at Savona for three years, and then (1812) at Fontainebleau! A meanest trick from the would-be rival of the Frankish Charles-the-Great.

Strange to say, Pope Leo XIII. is making the same political effort to-day to get the French Aristocracy and Gentry—these traditional and intimate supporters of the Catholic Church and Kings and Queens in Europe—to sustain and preserve Republicanism, exactly for the same motive as Pius VII. sustained and preserved the Imperialism of the bad man, who "turned" and "locked him up." Leo XIII. is the Head of his Church; and the French Aristocracy and Gentry, just like the English Catholic Aristocracy and Gentry, respect and obey him as their Head in matters SPIRITUAL. But in matters not spiritual— and the maintenance and preservation of Republicanism are indeed not spiritual matters—the French Aristocracy and Gentry may not bow down before the Pope's political opportunism towards the French Republic. Moreover, the French supporters of King and Queen and of the Royal Family of France to-day should take care to keep honourable and loyal to the Throne of the King of France; as both Pius VII. and Napoléon Bonaparte should have kept honourable and loyal to the legitimate successor of King Louis XVI. against external enemies and against internal disorder. To support the French anti-Catholic Republic, while attacking the Italian Catholic Royalty, seems an illogical hand-to-mouth opportunism at the Vatican; politicians call it ultramontanism. It is used by that portion of the Catholic Clergy who—in search of their own interest—do their best to trap their Catholic fellows into the snare of their high-sounding words and unctuous phrases, such as "Democracy is the back-bone of England!" and "the mission of the Church in England is through the social position of Catholics!" Such polite ecclesiastics are styled "*les épiscopables*" in France. Backslidings and schismatical movements within the Catholic Church, either on the Continent or in England, are caused by the Clergy's interference in civic and political contentions. See Italy (the Pope's own land), Austria, Spain, Ireland, America, and Belgium. Absolute neutrality is the Catholic Priest's best policy; my honorable parish priest tells me so. A married clergyman is

320th.—Theology in religion is what poisons are in food.

321st.—Toleration is one of the first rights of man. It is the first maxim of the gospel, since it is the first attribute of charity.

322nd.—To make use one day of a party, to attack it the next, whatever the pretext with which we may shield ourselves, is to betray it.

---

more excusable; *cela s'entend.* But France will "right" herself from her misdeeds and miseries in good time; "time and patience"—says the Eastern proverb—"change the mulberry leaf to satin." The French should be true to their Church and to their Royal Family as the English are to theirs. The flowing tide is rising with sweeping rapidity in favour of the French supporters of "King and Queen," and of the Royal Family of France. "Standing still" means not slipping back in their case. It may be statecraft for the Head of a Church to put his Communion on the side of the Democracy or common people, because he thinks common people may get the upper hand of Royalty and Aristocracy, like in France and more fully in America. But this uprising of Democracy in Germany and in England should be looked upon with suspicion by Europe, if not with hostility; the Latin-Celtic race need no German or English incentive; it is excitable enough already. And the siding of a Head of a Church with the common people against Crowned Heads is but a sore compromise politically, which must needs lead to Republicanism and the more serious misgrowth of Anarchy, from idle and factious men. Democracy is by birth and habit a body brutal, tyrannical, and unfit to govern themselves. The mass of Christians do not care a straw for the Pope; their Kings and Queens they love. To support the French Republic is an obvious and patent injustice towards European Royal Heads and Royal Families, politically speaking; to support the French Republic is an obvious and patent injustice towards Christianity, religiously speaking, because the effect of French Republicanism (its true name is the old FRENCH REVOLUTION) on Europe has been and is to inculcate the infidel unbelief among people that the religion of a nation is a matter of no political importance. This idea and judgment of mine about the noble science of Politics some may call impertinent interference and a coarse abuse of the Catholic Church. We can't please everybody, and I don't intend to try. History is facts, however, and by History I go and I stand. In the first place Republicanism goes against France as regards that nation's good "at home." Hear—strange from a Republican Official—what Professor COMBARIEU, the Principal Private Secretary to M. Loubet, President of the French Republic to-day, says in his HISTOIRE DE FRANCE:—"*La Révolution Française en définitive a créé en France là où il y avait des castes des partis et*

323rd.—A country like France can, and ought to, have a few houses for mad people, and call them trappists.*

324th.—God has placed work as the sentinel over virtue practising.

325th.—Odd people should never be controlled, providing they be harmless.

---

des débris ou noyaux de factions. Elle a suscité les convoitises de chacun ; elle a introduit l'indiscipline morale dans les esprits. Enfin, elle tend à remplacer le patriotisme par le cosmopolitisme. Ces faits expliquent bien des défaites et plus d'un abaissement." Is not Professor Combarieu's opinion, published by himself, the "best evidence" that Leo XIII. is feeling "nappy," à la Pius VII.? His Holiness is out of his reckoning, anyhow. Is not the best means of escaping this political epidemic to uphold strongly the standard of highest Monarchical and Aristocratic Rule of King and Queen ? It is. And is not the English Constitution the most rational type of that rule with eminent GENTLEMEN, above all suspicion, as Ministers of State and as Administrators, honourable and loyal to their Sovereign and Country ? It is. Like the Commonwealth of Cromwell, Republicanism and Imperialism—Siamese twins they are—are the caprice only of the fickle common people or Democracy. The French Republic, on the other hand, is an international nuisance to Europe, and scarce tolerable, except with distrust and apprehension, under the pressure of accident, or necessity political. It is an evil to be put up with out of pure deference to a prudential expedient ; but not to be recommended as a home duty nor as a lofty standard of political morals and manners. Such seem alone the natural conclusions I, for one, can draw from the Republican Professor Combarieu's dogmatic words. The Professor-Secretary is self-contradictory in plain truth and honesty. But his words, none the less, stand in my own favour as the vivid indication of a pressing need for France to vote, 1st, that, by the ancient and fundamental laws of the Realm, the Government of France was and ought to be by KING, PEERS, and COMMONS ; and, 2nd, that H.R.H. the Duc d'Orléans be invited to come and receive the Crown of his Royal father and ancestors, and to enter Paris at the head of the French Nobility and Gentry with the ROYAL FAMILY OF FRANCE—a Royal Family second to none in virtues, wisdom, and talent in Europe.—*Deum timeto, Regem honorato.* (L. E. H.)

* *Trappists* are an old order of monks, originally called "Cistercians" (from Citeaux, a monastery not far from Dijon), and Trappists from Trappe (la), a famous Abbey, founded in 1140, near Mortagne (Orne), reformed by Abbot de Rancé (1662), and whose monks kept the pledge of perpetual silence. Their supreme rule of conduct in their supernatural existence is the same as in the Army—and the safest one it is to get a soldier through :—*Omnes monachi magistram sequantur regulam.* Haughty Napoléon, living under pressure from

326th.—A throne is but a board covered in velvet.

327th.—Courage strengthens a throne, cowardice and infamy overthrow it; it is better to abdicate.

328th.—In times of trouble, all reason—even the reason of policy, the least indispensable—seems to become obscured with the destiny of the country.

---

a different world, was not expected to be so cautiously versed in the consideration of what Lord Salisbury calls "Ecclesiastical Literature." Napoléon appears at any rate to have entertained as phlegmatic a care for Trappists as Lord Salisbury does for Ecclesiastical faddists. To these two big men. "Theology in religion is what poisons are in food." (V. Part IV., *Thought* 320th.) I pass on to what I regard with greater interest and more practical.

To my Military Readers and other experts in Topography desirous to "kill two birds with one stone"—to know about Napoléon's Trappists *de visu*, and to get smart sketches—I suggest the short and useful excursion from Calais to Hazebrouck. Close by they will find the Mont-des-Cats, or Trappistine Abbey of Ste. Marie-du-Mont—a gem for draughtsmen and painters This is an exquisite and noble home of abbatical cloisters, dwelling supreme amidst the choicest scenes of landscape beauty. It stands on a mountain top, overtowering a most picturesque and sublime panorama on all sides. Military men who "go in" for the more exact and scientific delineation and description of the topographical class will bring back to England, I'm sure, none but fond regrets and tender recollections from their peaceful visit to Mont-des-Cats, which place is neither a "Synagogue of Satan" nor a "Leper Colony" beneath a visit from those two "old Gentlemen"—Napoléon and Lord Salisbury. Furthermore, the present Abbot or head monk—the Right Rev. Father Jérôme, O.C.R., a monk universally beloved and very popular, is an ex-military man; one of the distinguished fighters of the 1870-71 War. He is all-kindness to visitors. Through his courteous and brotherly *Père Hôtelier*, he likes strangers to relish the tasty food and drinks, which are the staple articles of consumption made by the artless Trappists for home and foreign markets, and which the Food and Drinks Adulteration Bill has come none too soon to protect rightly against swindling traders. The food and drinks I speak of are a chaste *beer*, brewed not with a false colouring ; true *butter*, not sophisticated heartlessly; a virtuous *cognac*, not degraded atrociously; single *bread*, not kneaded irreligiously with weevils; luscious *milk*, not *baptisé* puritanically. And, finally, it will make it clear to my readers, as it did to me, that Napoléon and Lord Salisbury are (s)trapping fellows, both born with the fondness of owning something broader than their own shoe ; but not born with too strong a note of the Trappist's fondness for his "*conventual* literature" *for Christ's sake* ! Strangely enough Napoléon it was who said "The surest way to remain poor is to be an honest man." The poverty of the *inops et pauper* is one of the three vows sworn to by the Monks of the Catholic Church. *Ergo*. . . (V. Part IV., *Thought* 242nd.)

L. E. H.

329th.—The most insupportable of tyrannies is that of inferiors.

330th.—Unity, good arrangements, and method, are the conditions without which, in architecture as in more important business, nothing can be fine or imposing.

331st.—The inevitable end of multiplied heads is to fade and to disappear for want of oneness.

332nd.—We often get in quicker by the back door than by the front.

333rd.—No political resolution is without excessive popular vengeance, when by any cause whatsoever the masses take a part in it.

334th.—Vices are necessary to the state of society, like storms to the atmosphere. If equilibrium is broken between good and evil, harmony ceases, and there is a revolution.

335th.—He who practices right, but in the hope of acquiring a great renown, is very near to vice.

336th.—There are vices and virtues which are only so by circumstances.

337th.—Victory is always to be praised, whether our luck or skill has lead us to it.

338th.—It is when leaving life, that we cling most to it.

339th.—Home life is the security of a good house; it assures the good name of the wife, the reliance of the husband, and keeps up friendliness and good manners.

340th.—The life of a happy man is a picture with a silver ground and some black stars. The life of an unhappy man is like a picture with a black ground and some gold stars.

341st.—The private life of a man is the reflector in which we read and gain useful information.

342nd.—Old men, who preserve the tastes of their youth, lose in consideration what they gain in ridicule.

343rd.—The herd seek out the great, not for their sake, but for their influence; and the latter welcome them out of vanity or need.

344th.—The herd measures the influence of a courtier by the number of his lacqueys; it judges the power of God by that of His priests.

Conclusion.

The English book called " Stories of Waterloo " we once read :—It is a foul and enduring slander against Napoléon-the-Great. These " Stories" fully bear out our own impression of painful surprise at some writers of the day in England (two or three characteristic Officers of the British Army especially). No doubt maddened with pain at the rising power of France again, in the teeth of the Jewish and Infidel ill wind, those pushful and resourceful men express their personal sufferings and disappointed ambition rather than the national feelings of Englishmen towards France and Napoléon. I feel unqualified to treat of the suggestive virtues of the Duke of Wellington, who proved himself as chivalrous and good-natured a friend to France and Paris—*95 out of every 100 Englishmen resemble the generous Duke there*—as butcher Blücher showed himself truly unfeeling, hostile and malevolent. However, it all lies in a nutshell : While a mean attempt has been often made to lower the Military character of the great French warrior who is now no more, we maintain that those who would libel Napoléon rob Wellington of half his glory. Clearly it is the proud boast of England's hero—this the Marlborough of the XIXth Century—that the subjugator of Europe fell before him ; 1st, not in the wave of his genius, but in the full possession of those martial talents which placed him foremost in the list of conquerors; 2nd, leading, too, that very army which had overthrown every power that had opposed it, and which was perfect in its discipline, flushed with recent success, and confident of approaching victory on the day on which the Duke of Wellington silenced Napoléon for ever. Personally I wonder at the wretched and helpless envy exhibited by certain Englishmen about the glory of Napoléon, and so industriously put before us by a man whose sole way to the fore has been by telling lies. "Lies have long legs," as the German saying is; and some think no harm can be done by forcing a few of these ugly toads into the Procrustean bed of facts. But they cannot shake our faith in Napoléon's military existence as an active, living, and vitalising force having made a tremendous lot for the military progressiveness of this century. War is no ideal. Most of civilians are apt to regard Napoléon as a foreign criminal, with a duplex dose of Adam's original guilt; and the serpent woman's credulous lagtag, skittish about sinister wars, must be reminded that Napoléon, if criminal, was a culprit precisely because he was so mortal, just like Bismarck. Mark Twain writes: "All things are mortal but the Jew." We are human things mortal-born. Soldiers of distinction are not produced on the downy bed of "fresh woods and pastures new" spread for the tales of love and courtship! Napoléon's Maxims and Thoughts have been a pleasant and dissecting study to me, however; and what and who was Napoléon appeared so entertaining to me because he is my ideal of a REAL GENERAL. Unfortunately for France, she is still suffering from the excesses of the French Revolution and from the inordinate ambitions of Napoléon which shed her best

blood, not only in France, but over Europe. France and England have fought fiercely, but always as *gentlemen*. The ancestors of some of my readers no doubt fought against France from early days to Dettingen and on to Waterloo; but I know that Englishmen have always had an admiration for French chivalry until France—untrue to herself—fell into the hands of Lawyers and the Political *canaille*. Those fearless representatives of English gallantry especially who have followed the French armies in several wars, who have had so many " bons camarades" in that glorious army, cannot entertain any feeling—they assure their English countrymen—but that of deep affection for it and of wonder and respect for its splendid officers and men. The intelligence of France seems ever to go slumbering under the curse of the spell laid on it by the evil enchanters called Republicans and Imperialists— these usurpers and the real enemies of freedom, truth and justice. It is because the bulk of them are the "gentlemen of the pavement" on the political field, and either Atheists or supporters of Philosophic Naturalism and Heathenism in the region of Creed. *Ça ne va pas durer.* Finally, I uphold with an honest and respectful obligation the wise and conscientious opinion of Field Marshal Von Moltke, who was the co-adjutor of Count Von Roon in drawing out the strategic programme for the Franco-German War:—" Whoever is well enough acquainted with the campaigns of Napoléon, and familiar enough with them to be able to recall at any moment the details of his battles and the movements that he ordered, has always in his hand the key to the movements proper to make under any given circumstances whatever."
—*Vive l'Armée!*

BOOKS OF REFERENCE ABOUT NAPOLÉON.

1. "Napoléon et les Cardinaux noirs, 1810 — 1814." By GEOFFROY DE GRANDMAISON.

2. "Histoire de la Chûte du Premier Empire, 1814—1815." By HENRY HOUSSAYE.

3. "Napoléon (Son caractère, son génie, son rôle historique.") By MARIUS SÉPET.

4. "La Société du Consulat et de l'Empire." By E. BERTIN.

5. "Napoléon (L'homme, le politique, l'orateur.") By A. GUILLOIS.

6. "Les Campagnes des Armées Françaises, 1792—1815." By CAMILLE VALLAUX.

7. "Généraux et Chefs de la Vendée militaire et de la Chouannerie (1793—1798—1815—1833)." By MM. DE LA SICOTIERE, JOUBERT, DE ROCHEBRUNE, etc.

8. "Vie du Comte Rostopchine, Gouverneur de Moscou, en 1812." By le Marquis A. DE SEGUR.

Fais que dois: advienne que pourra!

www.ingramcontent.com/pod-product-compliance
Lightning Source LLC
Chambersburg PA
CBHW070843160426
43192CB00012B/2284